God's
GREATER
GLORY

*Bringing Revival
to This
Generation*

KENNETH W. HAGIN

20 19 18 17 16 15 14   10 09 08 07 06 05 04

God's Greater Glory: Bringing Revival to This Generation
ISBN-13: 978-0-89276-744-1
ISBN-10: 0-89276-744-8

Copyright © 2004 Rhema Bible Church
AKA Kenneth Hagin Ministries, Inc.
All rights reserved.
Printed in USA

In the U.S. write:
Kenneth Hagin Ministries
P.O. Box 50126
Tulsa, OK 74150-0126
1-888-28-FAITH
rhema.org

In Canada write:
Kenneth Hagin Ministries of Canada
P.O. Box 335, Station D
Etobicoke (Toronto), Ontario
Canada M9A 4X3
1-866-70-RHEMA
rhemacanada.org

CONTENTS

A CRY FOR GLORY

I believe that God has spoken something to my heart and has given me a message that can change the lives of those who will hear it. God is doing great things in these last days, but I believe He wants to do even more. Throughout history, God has made known His desire to display His glory and His goodness to mankind. Many believers have experienced manifestations of the glory of God in various measures and have been blessed. But there is a *greater* glory that man has not seen, not in Bible times, nor in our time. And it's coming! But we have a part to play.

How do we cooperate with what God desires to do in the earth today concerning His glory? How do we enter in to what will undoubtedly be the greatest move of God the world has ever seen?

And what will we do with the greater glory that will be manifested in our midst?

In Acts chapter 17, we can read about certain people of Thessalonica in Paul's day who decried the rapid spreading of the salvation message and the staggering growth of the Christian faith. Threatened by this spiritual "movement," they accused those involved, among whom were Paul and Silas, saying, ". . . These that have turned the world upside down are come hither also" (Acts 17:6 *KJV*)!

Now, what they said wasn't intended as a compliment—to praise the zeal of Christ's disciples! But how strangely accurate a statement it was! It seems the Early Church as a whole was consumed with a zeal for God's glory.

Friend, we are a part of that Church today! God doesn't have two separate Churches; *we are all one Church of the Lord Jesus Christ!* And I believe wholeheartedly that in our day—as we usher into our midst the greater glory of God—His zeal will consume us, and it will be said of *us* throughout the earth: "These that have turned the world upside down are come hither also"!

What Does God Say About the Greater Glory?

To understand and have faith for the *"greater* glory," let's first look at the prophet Haggai's writings of God's glory in the past.

Haggai was one of the early "post-captivity" prophets and a contemporary of the prophet Zechariah. The message of the Book of Haggai comes from God directly to His people through the prophet. The reason for the message is that the people had been remiss in their rebuilding of God's temple.

They had been slow—*indifferent*, if you will—to rebuild the temple, and God had to send His messenger to remedy the situation.

The Book of Haggai contains only two chapters, but notice that in those two chapters, the words, "This is what the Lord says," are recorded in some form 19 times. Think about it! In 38 verses, some form of the phrase, "This is what the Lord says" is mentioned almost 20 times! I believe it is important, then, to find out just what the Lord was saying—to them and to *us*!

What Is the Glory of God?

First, let's look at one verse from Haggai, and then a passage of Scripture from Second Corinthians concerning the glory of God.

HAGGAI 2:9

9 " 'The glory of this present house will be greater than the glory of the former house,' says the Lord Almighty. 'And in this place I will grant peace,' declares the Lord Almighty."

2 CORINTHIANS 3:7–8

7 Now if the ministry that brought death, which was engraved in letters on stone, came with glory, so that the Israelites could not look steadily at the face of Moses because of its glory, fading though it was,

8 will not the ministry of the Spirit be even more glorious?

What is the glory of God? The *Holman Illustrated Bible Dictionary* defines the glory of God as the *weighty importance and shining majesty that accompany God's presence.*[1]

The *International Standard Bible Encyclopaedia* says the Hebrew word for God's glory *describes the form in which Jehovah (Yahweh) reveals Himself, or is the sign and manifestation of His presence.*[2]

Many times, we refer to the glory of God in such terms as "the power of God," "the Presence of God," the "Shekinah glory," and the "glory cloud" or "cloud of glory."

I saw the Charismatic Renewal begin and expand in the 1960s and '70s. And, with that revival, I saw certain groups come to the forefront in terms of being on fire with God's power and glory. Then I also saw some of those same groups die out and become only a shell of what they were in former years.

In these last days, we must not be complacent about the glory of God, just sort of sitting around and waiting to see what God will do next in the way of a move of the Spirit. We *must* get a revelation of what God wants *us* to do. We must be fully equipped to reach the lost and dying of the world with the Gospel of the Lord Jesus Christ. And we must be ready when the Lord Jesus returns for His glorious Church.

I am beginning to see that we who call ourselves Charismatic have let the glory of God wane in our midst. We—and I'm talking about all of us in the Body of Christ—must not do as the Israelites who lost their enthusiasm concerning the glory of God. They became apathetic in rebuilding God's temple, where God's glory would dwell in its fullness. And they became more interested in their own dwelling places, or in natural things—the affairs of everyday life.

HAGGAI 1:2–4

2 **This is what the Lord Almighty says: "These people say, 'The time has not yet come for the Lord's house to be built.'"**

3 **Then the word of the Lord came through the prophet Haggai:**

4 **"Is it a time for you yourselves to be living in your paneled houses, while this house** [speaking of the House of God, the temple] **remains a ruin?"**

Now at the time of this writing, the Israelites had returned from Babylonian captivity, and had already built houses for themselves. (God said in verse 4, "Is it time for you yourselves to be living in paneled houses while Mine remains a ruin?") However, some 16 years after their return, they had not yet rebuilt God's temple.

Now God is not against us living in nice houses. But it is more important that we build *His* house. Until we do—until we put first things *first* concerning the things of God—we are never going to see His greater glory.

What Does It Mean—*First Things First?*

One thing I believe many people need to change in their individual lives is an overemphasis on material things. We all need to get our eyes off ourselves and stop taking the attitude, "What's in it for us?" Instead, we should be asking ourselves the question, "What does *God* want?" and then count everything else as worthless in comparison to *His* will.

We need to let go of some things we've been holding on to, afraid that obeying God's perfect will might mean losing some earthly benefit. We must get our eyes off material things and on the things of God. I know you've heard it before, but it is a fundamental truth, so I'm going to say it again: We need to put first things *first*.

MATTHEW 6:33 (KJV)

33 But seek ye first the kingdom of God, and his righteousness; and all these things shall be added unto you.

If you read this verse in its context, you'll find that when Jesus said "all these things," He was talking about food and clothes—material things that the Gentiles, or the world, strives for and seeks after.

In Haggai, we read that the Israelites were planting and— yet when they sat down to eat, they didn't have enough.

HAGGAI 1:6

6 "You have planted much, but have harvested little. You eat, but never have enough. You drink, but never have your fill. You put on clothes, but are not warm. You earn wages, only to put them in a purse with holes in it."

What was the problem? The Israelites were sowing. Well, isn't it good and right to sow? Certainly, it is. In fact, it is thoroughly scriptural. But they were not putting God's interests ahead of their own. *They were not putting first things first!*

Jesus Himself said, in effect, "If you'll seek first the Kingdom of God, all these things you've been seeking after will be added to you." He didn't say you'd have to strive for them. In fact, He told us in the verses leading up to verse 33 that we shouldn't be anxious about our needs being met (Matt. 6:25).

Well, what is "the Kingdom of God and His righteousness" that we are supposed to be seeking? Basically, it's God's will, *His way*. For example, after they'd been released from captivity God told the Israelites to rebuild His house, His temple. Well, to seek first His Kingdom and His righteousness would have meant obedience. It would have meant to set aside natural, earthly things for the time being in order to take care of His interests. Instead, they sought first their own well-being and left the task He'd assigned to them undone. They *intended* to rebuild the temple, but they wanted to do it when it was convenient for *them*, not when *God* wanted it done.

What can we learn from the Israelites in Haggai's day? It seems they became focused on themselves and on material things. In the process, they put off rebuilding the house of God. And if we're not careful today, we, too, can become more involved with our personal lives than with the things of God.

It seems that some today have become indifferent to the things of God and to His will and plan for their lives. Spiritual things are no longer a priority. They are more interested in furthering themselves than they are in furthering God's plan and His work, ushering in His glory, and the return of His Son.

But we have a divine commission to reach a lost and dying world with the message that Jesus Christ gave His life so that they might have life, and have it more abundantly (John 10:10).

If we are going to experience the greater glory—the glory that will be greater than that of the former house (Hag. 2:9)—we're going to have to do something about it. We can't just rock along and be satisfied with the status quo.

A Place to Start

So where do we start? In our own heart. We start by having a right attitude in our heart, and placing a high priority on God and the things of God. We start by holding the treasures of Heaven as weightier than natural, material things.

As I said, God is not against His children having things and living in material, financial wealth, and prosperity. I believe in divine prosperity, and I believe that it belongs to us as believers; it is one of our redemptive blessings and rights. But if we're not careful, we can become more interested in the prosperity God gives than in God Himself. And we can grow cold spiritually. We can grow numb and indifferent to spiritual things by becoming over-concerned with material things.

When we begin to seek *things* more than we seek the Kingdom of God and His righteousness (Matt. 6:33), we become out of balance. When we over-emphasize financial prosperity and underemphasize the Kingdom of God and the things of God, we are headed for the spiritual junk heap. When we walk that path, we will not experience God's greater glory.

I'm not saying a person isn't saved if he's preoccupied with money and material things. But I am saying that he's not going to *walk* in God's best if he doesn't *seek* His best. What did Jesus tell us to seek? He said, "Seek ye first the kingdom of God, and his righteousness; and all these things shall be added unto you" (Matt. 6:33 *KJV*).

I am not against material prosperity. It's scriptural, and it should certainly have its place in our lives. God desires that our every need be met and that we grow in financial prosperity, even as our soul prospers (3 John 2). I believe that we should have the material things that God has promised us. But too many people are going overboard. "Gimme, gimme, gimme" has become the essence of their prayer life. They are more caught up in *the things God gives* than they are in *God the Giver*.

God has blessed me and my family tremendously over the years. But I can honestly say that if I had to choose between those material things and the blessing of God's fellowship and His Spirit upon me, *I would choose God!* I would give up those things in a minute.

"Why?" someone might ask. "Didn't God bless you with those things to begin with?"

Yes, He did. And the same God who blessed me with the material blessings that I possess can bless me again if I lost them all tomorrow. But, on the other hand, if I lost the anointing tomorrow, all of my earthly possessions could not get it back for me.

Some Christians go overboard when it comes to the message of prosperity. In my opinion, they push the envelope too far. We saw the same thing happen in the Healing Revival of the 1940s and '50s. Certain men who were anointed by the power of God and were mightily used of God in the healing ministry missed it in the area of money. I've seen with my own eyes instances in which the power of God would move in a service, and these ministers would immediately get up and begin taking up an offering.

The people in those meetings were so blessed by the Spirit of God, they willingly gave. But, sadly, that money often went straight to the minister holding the meeting. He'd use it all, or most of it, to buy himself a new car or some other item of luxury.

We as ministers of the Gospel, and even as Christian lay people, need to be careful when it comes to money so that we don't sell out what we have with God for the material blessings of this world. I'm not saying we should accept poverty and lack—not at all! There's nothing wrong with living well and enjoying the prosperity that Jesus bought for us in His death, burial, and resurrection. But when we become more interested in prosperity and in material things than in the Giver of prosperity, there is a danger.

A Question of Focus

As I said, I believe God wants His children to have the best (Isa. 1:19). But the balance between natural, material things and the things of the Spirit is *focus*. According to Haggai, the Israelites had lost their focus on God and on spiritual things. And in getting caught up in their own affairs and the things of interest to them personally, they forsook the privilege of God's glory in worship.

I think we can say that, in a sense, what we see in the Book of Haggai is a prophetic picture of the Church today. In Haggai, we see a people who had made themselves their priority. They were not showing the reverence toward God and toward spiritual things that they should have shown. There is danger of that happening in the Church today, and that is why I'm writing this book. There is a move of the Spirit that will be lost to us in this generation if we fail to heed the Word of God and the prophets of old.

But I am believing to see greater and greater manifestations of God's glory! The truth is very simple: As we focus our attention on God and on the things of God, we will experience more of Him. The opposite is true too. If our focus and attention is on natural things, we will have fewer and fewer experiences with the glory of God.

We must prepare ourselves for this greater glory. We must rid ourselves of wrong attitudes, of our lust for material gain, and of anything that would hinder us from participating in this great move of God and experiencing manifestations of His greater glory!

The following is a word from the Lord that came forth as I ministered along this line in a meeting.

Prepare yourself, because there is a day coming . . .

Prepare yourself. Prepare yourself. Prepare yourself.

As John the Baptist went out and prepared the way [for] the Lord Jesus Christ,

I am preparing the way [for] this revival of greater glory. . . .

Get yourself ready, because the move of God is on its way.

And the end of all things is at hand. . . .

So let us consecrate ourselves afresh and anew and ask of the Lord fresh oil, that the anointing may flow and be evident to many. Though times may seem difficult, we should take up our cross and follow Him. We should obey Him in everything. He is the One who sees ahead, who goes before us, and who can be trusted with our very lives.

Friend, we each have a work to do! The Spirit of God is within us and upon us to accomplish our task. And He desires to manifest Himself as never before in our midst and in the presence of the whole world. So let us seize the opportunity to obey God and to cooperate with the flow of His Spirit. Let us seek God as never before so that we can step out fearlessly and proclaim His Gospel with signs following—so that we can take our place in this great ingathering of souls throughout the earth!

[1] Trent C. Butler, Chad Brand, Charles Draper, and Archie England, eds., *Holman Illustrated Bible Dictionary* (Nashville: Holman Bible Publishers, 2003), 655.

[2] James Orr, gen. ed., *International Standard Bible Encyclopaedia* (Chicago: Howard-Severance Co., 1915), vol. 2, 1236.

Chapter 2

GOD'S TEMPLE TODAY
The Display of His Splendor

If we ever needed a greater measure of God's glory, it is today. The Bible has predicted certain things that we would see in the last days, and we are seeing some of those unfortunate events unfolding in our day. The Bible also says that the spiritual condition of some will wax worse and worse. Second Timothy 3:1–4 even lists characteristics of those walking in darkness in the last days.

2 TIMOTHY 3:1–4

1 **But mark this: There will be terrible times in the last days.**

2 **People will be lovers of themselves, lovers of money, boastful, proud, abusive, disobedient to their parents, ungrateful, unholy,**

3 **without love, unforgiving, slanderous, without self-control, brutal, not lovers of the good,**

4 **treacherous, rash, conceited, lovers of pleasure rather than lovers of God.**

But time and time again in the Word of God, we also see references to increased manifestations of the glory of God. We understand that God's people were designed and created to display His mighty power and glory throughout history. And we who are alive today on the earth are no less destined to display His glory—His awesome splendor and majesty.

It is just as important to discover why the blessings and glory of God are not being manifested as they should as it is to discover how to position ourselves to experience the greater glory. For example, we've already looked at the following passage in which the Lord plainly spells out the reason for His people's lack of blessing in their lives:

HAGGAI 1:3-6,9

3 . . . the word of the Lord came through the prophet Haggai:

4 "Is it a time for you yourselves to be living in your paneled houses, while this house remains a ruin?"

5 Now this is what the Lord Almighty says: "Give careful thought to your ways.

6 You have planted much, but have harvested little. You eat, but never have enough. You drink, but never have your fill. You put on clothes, but are not warm. You earn wages, only to put them in a purse with holes in it."

9 "You expected much, but see, it turned out to be little. What you brought home, I blew away. Why?" declares the Lord Almighty. "Because of my house, which remains a ruin, while each of you is busy with his own house."

The house God referred to is the temple that Solomon had built—the one that was destroyed when the Babylonians invaded and destroyed the city of Jerusalem. God said, "You expected much, but it turned out to be little, because My house remains ruined while you are busy with your own houses" (v. 9).

But if you'll read further, you'll find that God then encouraged the people by promising them future glory and blessings if they obeyed Him by rebuilding His house, His temple. So in the midst of correcting them, God also gave them hope for their future.

HAGGAI 2:9

9 " 'The glory of this present house will be greater than the glory of the former house,' says the Lord Almighty. 'And in this place I will grant peace,' declares the Lord Almighty."

Isn't that just like God! We need to realize that God desires to pour out His Spirit and manifest His glory more than we want Him to!

The first part of Haggai 2:9 says, " 'The glory of this present house will be greater than the glory of the former house . . . .' " In the "former house," the people saw and experienced the glory of God. Well, what about us today? Where is that greater glory that the prophet Haggai spoke of?

2 CORINTHIANS 3:7-11

7 Now if the ministry that brought death, which was engraved in letters on stone, came with glory, so that the Israelites could not look steadily at the face of Moses because of its glory, fading though it was,

8 will not the ministry of the Spirit be even more glorious?

9 If the ministry that condemns men is glorious, how much more glorious is the ministry that brings righteousness!

10 For what was glorious has no glory now in comparison with the surpassing glory.

11 And if what was fading away came with glory, HOW MUCH GREATER IS THE GLORY OF THAT WHICH LASTS!

You see, in the Old Testament, the glory of God was manifested only in certain places at certain times through certain channels. When the glory of God was manifested, it was usually only upon the prophets, priests, or kings. But according to First Corinthians 3:16, *every* born-again child of God is the temple of the Holy Spirit.

1 CORINTHIANS 3:16 (KJV)

16 Know ye not that YE ARE THE TEMPLE OF GOD, and that the Spirit of God dwelleth in you?

1 CORINTHIANS 3:16 (Amplified)

16 Do you not discern and understand that you [the whole church at Corinth] are God's temple (His sanctuary), and that God's Spirit has His permanent dwelling in you [to be at home in you, collectively as a church and also individually]?

According to this verse, individual Christians—members of the Body of Christ—are God's temple. Paul wrote to the Church at Corinth, "You are God's temple." And since the people in the Church at Corinth were God's temple, we in the Church today are God's temple. *We are God's temple!*

In your local church building, you may find cement, steel, wood, bricks, stone, mortar, and so forth. However, although that church is dedicated to the propagation of the Gospel, the power and glory of God do not reside in that building or in any other building! The glory of God is in *you and me*, and when we walk into church, the glory of God comes in *with us*.

Therefore, if we want the power of God to manifest in our midst, we're going to have to do something both individually and collectively for God to move corporately in the local church body and in the Body of Christ at large as a whole.

Well, what must we do? First, we must cultivate and maintain a greater hunger for the things of God and for a move of His Spirit. We must continually worship Him in Spirit and in truth. And we must hold fast to His Word and to the truth we know without compromise. We must preach and teach the Word with greater and greater fervency! *And we must show reverence for the Presence of God in our midst.* (In the following chapters, I will teach in detail on nine keys to experiencing God's greater glory.)

The Consequences of Neglecting Spiritual Things

We read previously that the word of the Lord had come through the prophet Haggai to God's people, saying, *"Is it a time for you yourselves to be living in your paneled houses, while this house* [speaking of the house of God, the temple] *remains a ruin?"* (Hag. 1:4). We know that the Israelites had neglected the rebuilding of the temple. Verses 5 through 7 give us a picture of the consequences of their neglect.

HAGGAI 1:5–7

5 Now this is what the Lord Almighty says: "Give careful thought to your ways.

— 19 —

6 You have planted much, but have harvested little. You eat,
but never have enough. You drink, but never have your
fill. You put on clothes, but are not warm. You earn wages,
only to put them in a purse with holes in it."

7 This is what the Lord Almighty says: "Give careful thought
to your ways."

Notice in verses 5 and 7, the Lord Almighty says, ". . . Give
careful thought to your ways." The *King James Version* says,
". . . Consider your ways." Now, in our modern language, we
might interpret that as "Wake up and smell the coffee!"

You've heard that saying, haven't you? If someone is
seemingly oblivious or ignorant and unaware of some obvi-
ous truth, someone might say to him or her, "Wake up and
smell the coffee!"

A Wakeup Call for God's People Today

That is what God was saying to the children of Israel, and
I believe He is saying that to us today. Remember, *we* are
God's temple, His house. And we need to consider and give
careful thought to our ways.

Let's look more closely at Haggai 1:6.

HAGGAI 1:6

6 "You have planted much, but have harvested little. You
eat, but never have enough. You drink, but never have
your fill. You put on clothes, but are not warm. You earn
wages, only to put them in a purse with holes in it."

There are many in the Church today who are planting a
lot in the area of finances, but they're not reaping very much.

They don't have enough to get by on. They are in lack. God could be saying to them, "Give careful thought to your ways."

If that fits you, I'm not saying this to be mean. I'm saying it because the good news is, it's not too late to begin considering your ways and building up the spiritual house of God by putting spiritual things first.

As I said, it all has to do with our focus and with the attitude of our heart. The Bible talks about our need to guard our heart (Prov. 4:23). And one of the things we have to guard against is becoming preoccupied with natural things. The house of God that Haggai referred to was the temple where God's Spirit dwelt. But we've already seen that today individually and collectively, *we* are the temple where God's Spirit dwells.

By becoming preoccupied with natural things, the Israelites neglected God's temple. But too, we can become preoccupied with natural things and neglect the things of God, the furthering of His Kingdom, and His plan and purpose on the earth.

God told the Israelites in Haggai 1:6 (and it can apply to us too) what happens when you neglect spiritual things and fail to keep Him as your priority. This verse might give some indication, why some people are quoting God's Word, but don't seem to be getting anywhere with their faith.

HAGGAI 1:6

6 **"You have planted much, but have harvested little. You eat, but never have enough. You drink, but never have**

your fill. You put on clothes, but are not warm. You earn wages, only to put them in a purse with holes in it."

In modern-day language, this verse might read, "You're working your fingers to the bone, but it doesn't amount to anything."

Have you ever felt that way? I think most of us have at one time or another. Well, what does the Word of God say to do? It tells us to consider or to give careful thought to our ways (vv. 5,7).

From time to time, we need to ask ourselves why we're doing the things we do for the Kingdom of God. Do we volunteer to work in our church just to be seen by people or to please others? Or are we doing it for God? Do we give offerings just to receive material blessings in return, or do we do it from a heart of love and gratitude for the blessings He has given us?

Now, I realize that the Word of God says that we will be blessed as we give. And because God said it, we should expect it to happen in our lives. But is receiving something from Him our only motive? I remember one fellow came up to me after a service once, and he was very upset. "I'm not getting a return on anything I'm giving," he complained.

I asked him, "Why are you giving?"

"Well, so I can receive."

Yet, because the Word appeared not to be working for him, the man was irate. He didn't have a humble attitude of love for the Lord. His attitude was wrong, and if *getting* was his only motive for *giving*, then his motive was wrong too.

Now, God can bless some people in spite of their actions at times, because they are ignorant about what they're doing. But others are not ignorant; their motives are wrong.

Some people come to a special meeting, and they think they have to have a front-row seat in the church. Well, what is their motive? Is it to get as close as they can so they don't miss anything the minister says or does, because they're hungry for God? Or do they just want special treatment and to be seen by others? You see, it all has to do with the attitude of the heart.

I always ask myself before I start to do something in ministry, *Am I doing this for my benefit or for the Kingdom of God?* You see, if we're going to experience the greater glory, we're going to have to make some heart changes. We're going to have to consider our ways. And as I said, I'm not saying this to be mean or to condemn anyone. Remember, after God told the people through Haggai to consider their ways, He told them what to do to change the condition they found themselves in. He told them how they could obey Him and turn some things around. And the Bible says they did it willingly (Hag. 1:12).

HAGGAI 1:8

8 "Go up into the mountains and bring down timber and build the house, so that I may take pleasure in it and be honored," says the Lord.

In His message through the prophet Haggai, God explained to the people why they weren't being blessed as they should have been and as He desired. But He not only told them what they were doing wrong, He also told them exactly what to do to begin rectifying the situation: "Go up into the mountains and bring down timber and build the house . . ." (Hag. 1:8). You can't get much more explicit than that!

If we're not already doing so, it's not too late for us to begin building up God's temple—to build up ourselves individually and the Church corporately—for the glory of God. Through Haggai, God was telling the Israelites they needed to change their priorities so that the glory of God could return. They needed to change their focus from *themselves* and what *they* thought was more important to *God* and what *He* thought was more important. He told them, in effect, "You take care of My house, and I will take care of yours."

That applies to us today. We all must be busy about the Father's business, doing what He wants us to do so we will be ready to receive a greater measure of the glory and power of God in our lives.

The Greater Glory Is Manifested Based on Our Desire for the Things of God

Previously, I mentioned some things we need to do to usher in the greater glory. One of the things I mentioned was the need to cultivate and to maintain a greater hunger for a move of God's Spirit on the earth. In other words, we have to *want* it!

The Israelites needed to stir themselves up to *want* God's glory to return to His temple. God had delivered them from captivity. They had returned to their own land and had built their homes. But after 16 years, they still had not rebuilt the temple! God used Haggai to speak to them so that they would stir themselves up and finish the task they had been assigned to do.

Once the Israelites understood where they had missed it, they began to obey the Lord's command to rebuild the temple and to begin putting first things *first* (Hag. 1:12–14).

HAGGAI 2:6,7

6 "This is what the Lord Almighty says: 'In a little while I will once more shake the heavens and the earth, the sea and the dry land.

7 I will shake all nations, and the desired of all nations will come, and I will fill this house with glory,' says the Lord Almighty."

Remember that back then, the glory of God dwelt in the temple in the Holy Place, the Holy of Holies. But where does God's glory reside today? In the Body of Christ. In *us*!

If there is going to be a manifestation of the greater glory today, you and I are going to have to do something about it. It wasn't God's responsibility to rebuild the temple in Jerusalem. That task had been assigned to God's people. And, today, it is our responsibility, not God's, to stir ourselves up to put Him first and to esteem spiritual things over earthly, material things.

What am I saying to you? I'm saying when God deals with us (and I believe that He is dealing with us now), there's going to be a shaking of our priorities. And the greater glory is going to come! There will be a greater visitation of God's power and Presence than we have seen yet. But it will come with a price—the price of our time and our earnest desire to seek His face and to know Him! It's the price of our obedience to move when He says to move, and to sit still when He says to sit still. Will you pay the price?

Do you want to see the glory of this present house be greater than that of the former house (Hag. 2:9)? God is letting us know that we need to change some things so that the glory of God can be manifested in our lives. God wants His house—that's *you and me*—to be filled with His glory. He wants the glory of the latter house, the present-day house, to be even greater than it was in the heyday of Solomon's temple.

We've already established that the glory of God in our day is not going to be manifested in a physical building per se—apart from us, the Body of Christ. No, *we* are God's building, His temple, the house in which He dwells. And He is going to manifest Himself in and through us.

We call our local church "the house of God." But in a literal sense, that is simply not true. It is called that because that's where we go to worship God corporately. But there is no glory present in the building itself. If you don't believe me, just try walking through your church sanctuary or auditorium at three o'clock in the morning when it's dark and empty! I've been inside our church late at night with just a flashlight, and it's an eerie feeling to be there alone in the dark.

Back when I traveled with my dad as a young boy, visiting ministers usually stayed in the parsonage with the pastor's family. There weren't a lot of hotels then like there are now. Sometimes the pastor's kids had to give up their rooms for the visiting minister, and all the kids would go next door and sleep in the church. I have slept many a night in church buildings, so I know firsthand that even a church can be a scary place at night!

"Why?" someone asked. "I thought the local church was called the house of God?"

The local church is called the house of God in the sense that it is dedicated for the plan and purpose of God—for the propagation of the Gospel. But as we've seen, God Himself does not reside in a building; He lives in us!

We are God's building, the house in which He dwells. And I believe that we will be seen in these last days as the display of His majestic splendor in the earth when He manifests His greater glory in our midst!

Chapter 3

WITNESSES OF THE GLORY

Even in Charismatic circles, I think that we in the Body of Christ today have lost some of the fervency and fire with which the Charismatic Renewal began in the '60s and '70s. Along with the Charismatic Renewal, greater emphasis began to be placed on the integrity of God's Word and on making faith "confessions," or exercising one's faith in line with God's Word. But, over time, we let some of those truths get away from us, too; we have not practiced them as we should have.

In the 1950s, God told my father, Rev. Kenneth E. Hagin, "Go teach My people faith," and Dad was faithful to do that up to the time of his passing in 2003. Even when it was more popular to teach something "new" in the way of spiritual revelation, my dad kept at it; he kept teaching on faith. He did what God told him to do. If he hadn't done it, some invaluable truths would have been lost to our generation. Dad also taught some invaluable truths concerning the move of the

Spirit of God that we need to hold fast to so that they will not be lost to us.

As I've studied Church history, I have observed that when there is a great new move of God on the earth, such as the Healing Revival, people's enthusiasm begins to wane after a time. Some even pull away from the move of the Spirit that they've witnessed and experienced for themselves. I see that happening today with some pastors trying to dictate to the Holy Spirit when He can and cannot move in their churches.

A New Wave of Revival

I believe that we are on the brink of a revival of greater glory! We are right on the edge of a new revival that's going to sweep in and bless humankind as we've never seen before.

We often hear of new moves of God's Spirit compared to waves of water. The Holy Spirit in Scripture is often referred to as water. And, certainly, throughout history, there has been an ebb and flow to the various moves of the Spirit of God.

Well, there is a new wave coming! In one sense, it is a new wave; yet in another sense, it is not a new wave. It's a *different* wave in that it follows and is higher than the one before. But it's the *same* in that it is part of the same water.

Of course, not everyone is going to flow with this new revival. Although many are hungry for God and the things of God and are crying out in prayer for more of Him, others are not yielding to the promptings of the Spirit to prepare and position themselves for this new move.

When God does something new in the Body of Christ, some pull back from it because, while they ascribe to believing in the power of God, to them it's only something written on paper, not something we're actually supposed to experience.

In the late 1970s as I traveled with Dad as crusade director, it was not uncommon to see the glory cloud—the Shekinah glory of God—roll in to those services. And I've been in meetings in which you could actually hear and feel wind blowing in to the service—and I'm talking about churches with no air conditioning and with no fans running! (In Scripture, the Holy Spirit is also referred to as wind [Acts 2:2].)

Those were manifestations of the power and glory of God. And because we're living in the last days, we need to experience more manifestations of God's glory and become more acquainted with His moving so that we can flow with it and cooperate with Him to reap the last-day harvest of souls in the earth.

Many people talk excitedly about accounts they've heard about from the revival of the '50s when people who had been confined to wheelchairs and stretchers would get up and walk during healing meetings. "Those were great times!" they'll say.

While it's good to reminisce about the good things God has done in the past, we should also be looking with anticipation for even greater outpourings of God's glory today.

What is the revival of the "greater glory" going to bring? I believe it will consist of elements of all the great moves of God in the past. There will be outpourings of the Holy Spirit that will transcend denominational lines, and there will be tremendous healings and other manifestations of the power of God. It will be an unparalleled last-days revival.

Someone asked, "Well, how do you know these are the last days?"

I didn't say that I know the exact time at which Jesus will return. The Bible says that only God knows the day and the hour of that great event (Mark 13:32). But all you have to do to understand that we are living in the last days is to look at everything that's happening in the world around us—wars, rumors of wars, earthquakes, famines, and so forth. The signs of the times are evident. But we can look for Jesus' return with great rejoicing, because of the promise of the greater glory. (See Mark 13:3–8.)

The Bible says that the latter glory will be greater than the former glory. Haggai 2:9 says, "'The glory of this present house will be greater than the glory of the former house,' says the Lord Almighty . . ." (Hag. 2:9).

Let's look at the glory of the former house and "reminisce," if you will, about some of the great things God did that are recorded in His Word.

In looking at the glory of the former house, we see in the Book of Exodus that on at least one occasion, the glory cloud covered the Tent of Meeting, and the glory of the Lord filled the tabernacle. Moses could not even enter the Tent of Meeting because the cloud had settled upon it!

EXODUS 40:34,35

34 Then the cloud covered the Tent of Meeting, and the glory of the Lord filled the tabernacle.

35 Moses could not enter the Tent of Meeting because the cloud had settled upon it, and the glory of the Lord filled the tabernacle.

Now let's look at the glory in the Book of Leviticus.

LEVITICUS 9:5,6,23

5 They took the things Moses commanded to the front of the Tent of Meeting, and the entire assembly came near and stood before the Lord.

6 Then Moses said, "This is what the Lord has commanded you to do, SO THAT THE GLORY OF THE LORD MAY APPEAR TO YOU."

23 Moses and Aaron then went into the Tent of Meeting. When they came out, they blessed the people; AND THE GLORY OF THE LORD APPEARED TO ALL THE PEOPLE.

As I said, in some of Dad's revival meetings, the cloud of glory would actually manifest in a service, and certain people in the congregation would see it. But here in Leviticus chapter 9, it says, ". . . the glory of the Lord appeared to *all* the people" (v. 23).

Then in Acts chapter 2 where we read about the Day of Pentecost, it implies that everyone present heard the "wind" and saw the "tongues of fire."

ACTS 2:1-3

1 When the day of Pentecost came, they were all together in one place.

2 Suddenly a sound like the blowing of a violent wind came from heaven and filled the whole house where they were sitting.

3 They saw what seemed to be tongues of fire that separated and came to rest on each of them.

Let's look at yet another passage to illustrate my point that throughout the Bible, manifestations of God's glory were often experienced by *all* who were present, not just a few.

2 CHRONICLES 7:1–3

1 When Solomon finished praying, fire came down from heaven and consumed the burnt offering and the sacrifices, and the glory of the Lord filled the temple.

2 The priests could not enter the temple of the Lord because the glory of the Lord filled it.

3 WHEN ALL THE ISRAELITES SAW THE FIRE COMING DOWN AND THE GLORY OF THE LORD ABOVE THE TEMPLE, they knelt on the pavement with their faces to the ground, and they worshiped and gave thanks to the Lord, saying, "He is good; his love endures forever."

Notice that *all* the people, not just a few, saw the manifestation of the glory of God.

I'm looking forward to the days when everyone present in a meeting—not just the minister or a few people in the congregation—will see and experience manifestations of the glory of God such as those witnessed in these passages.

There are many kinds of manifestations of the Presence of God. We read about people hearing what sounded like wind blowing (Acts 2:2). Others, including myself, can tell of feeling a gentle breeze in services when the glory of God was in manifestation. Some have even described the manifestation of the Spirit as a sweet-smelling fragrance.

Pentecostal Christians also talk of manifestations of the glory of God that left everyone present motionless and statue-like under the power of God. Once in the course of her ministry in the late nineteenth and early twentieth centuries, Sister Maria Woodworth-Etter had such an experience. Although she had fallen into "trances" under the power of the Spirit before, in this particular meeting, she went into a trance and stood as still as a statue *for three days* under a powerful manifestation of the Spirit of God!

After three days, she came out of it, and it's told that many were born again, accepting Jesus as their Savior as a result of this incident.

Over the years, we've seen glimpses of spectacular manifestations such as this one. But when this greater glory is revealed, manifestations like this won't come in bits and pieces. There will come a revival that encompasses the entire Church of the Lord Jesus Christ. You won't just be hearing about the experiences of others—you will be participating in the glory yourself!

I believe the time is coming when everyone present in a service will see a manifestation of the glory of God and fall flat on their faces under the power of God. I also believe that there will be meetings in which no healing line will need to be formed for the sick. But every sick person in that service, including those bound to wheelchairs, will rise up healed and whole by the power of Almighty God!

During the Healing Revival of 1947 through 1958, some of these things happened in meetings held by various ministers.

Many people were healed spontaneously, en masse, without anyone laying his or her hands on them to receive healing. They were healed by a spectacular manifestation of the power of God.

We sometimes hear of this happening in mass meetings overseas. When the truth of the risen Savior and Healer is proclaimed, thousands receive Him into their hearts and thousands are spontaneously healed in body as they hear—maybe for the first time—that God is a good God, that He loves people, and that He wants to see them blessed and made whole.

I've been in a few meetings like that myself in Africa. Thousands would begin to raise their hands at once, and throughout the crowd, we'd see ripples of clamoring as those who were sick, blind, and maimed were suddenly healed. One by one, I've seen many of those delivered by God's power walk across the platform, testifying, "I couldn't walk, but now I can walk and run perfectly!" "I was blind, but now I can see!" "I couldn't hear, but now I have perfect hearing!"

We've heard of and witnessed smatterings of God's outpouring throughout the world. But there is coming a time when manifestations such as these will be happening all the time! God has promised that there would be greater works (John 14:12)—and greater works we shall see! Are you ready?

The Acts of the Early Church: An Unfinished Book

The Book of Acts—The Acts of the Apostles—was written about the Early Church by Luke, who also wrote the Gospel of Luke. In fact, some call it "The Acts of the Early Church."

What were the acts of the Early Church? They were actually acts of the Spirit of God manifested to bless people and set them free.

Consider the following acts of the Holy Ghost through certain individuals in the Early Church. These acts bear further witness to the glory of God in the age in which we are living today.

- **In Acts 2:1–4**, believers were baptized in the Holy Ghost.

- **In Acts 3:1–11**, the lame man at the gate called Beautiful was healed.

- **In Acts 4:23–31**, believers at a prayer meeting were filled with the Holy Spirit, and the building where they were assembled was shaken.

- **In Acts 5:1–11**, there was a fearful display of God's judgment in the case of Ananias and Sapphira.

- **In Acts 5:12–16**, miraculous signs and wonders, salvations, healings, and deliverances were wrought by the hands of the apostles.

- **In Acts 5:18 and 19**, the disciples were supernaturally released from prison.

- **In Acts 6:8**, Stephen did great wonders and miracles by the Spirit of God.

- **In Acts 8:5–24**, Philip preached Christ in Samaria, and, through Philip, God wrought miracles, deliverances, healings, and salvations there. Peter also spoke to Simon by the Spirit of God.

- **In Acts 8:39 and 40**, Philip was supernaturally translated from one place to another.

- **In Acts 9:1–9**, Saul was miraculously converted on the road to Damascus.

- **In Acts 9:10–18**, Saul's blind eyes were opened when Ananias laid his hands on him.

- **In Acts 9:32–35**, In Lydda, Peter healed a paralytic who'd been lame for eight years.

- **In Acts 9:36–40**, God used Peter to raise Dorcas from the dead in Joppa.

- **In Acts 10:1–6**, Cornelius had an angelic vision.

- **In Acts 10:9–16**, Peter also had a vision in which God instructed him to go to Cornelius' house.

- **In Acts 10:44–46**, the Holy Spirit fell on Cornelius' household, and they were all saved and baptized in the Holy Ghost.

- **In Acts 11:27 and 28**, Agabus prophesied about future world events.

- **In Acts 12:3–11**, Peter was miraculously delivered from prison.

- **In Acts 12:20–23**, Herod was supernaturally judged by God.

- **In Acts 13:1–3**, God gave supernatural direction to ministers gathered to pray and minister to the Lord.

- **In Acts 13:6–12**, Paul supernaturally dealt with an opposer of the faith at Paphos.

- **In Acts 14:3**, God did signs and wonders by the hands of Paul and Barnabas.

- **In Acts 14:8–10**, a lame man was healed at Lystra as he heard Paul preach.

- **In Acts 16:6–10**, Paul received a supernatural plea for help in a vision.

- **In Acts 16:16–18**, Paul delivered a girl from the demon of fortune-telling.

- **In Acts 16:19–34**, Paul and Silas were miraculously delivered from prison, and the jailer's entire house received Christ.

- **In Acts 18:9 and 10**, Paul received a message of comfort from God in a vision.

- **In Acts 19:1–6,** believers were baptized in the Holy Spirit at Ephesus.

- **In Acts 19:11 and 12**, God wrought extraordinary miracles by the hands of Paul.

- **In Acts 20:7–12**, At Troas, Paul raised a young man from the dead.

- **In Acts 21:4**, believers urged Paul by the Spirit not to go to Jerusalem.

- **In Acts 21:10 and 11**, Agabus prophesied to Paul about the future.

- **In Acts 23:11**, Paul had an angelic vision.

- **In Acts 27:23–25**, Paul received another angelic vision and a message of good cheer.

- **In Acts 28:3–6**, Paul was supernaturally unharmed by a poisonous snake bite.

- **In Acts 28:7–9**, Paul laid hands on Publius' father and other sick folk on the island of Melita (Malta), and they were healed.

I have named at least 36 supernatural manifestations of the Holy Spirit accounted for in the Book of Acts. What were some of the characteristics of the Early Church that caused them to witness such spectacular events of the Spirit? For one, they maintained themselves in the Presence of God. They maintained their fervency and their devotion to Him.

Just a few months before the passing of my father, I spoke with him about some of these acts of the apostles and of the Early Church. He pointed out something very interesting to me. The essence of what he said was this: "Everybody thinks the Book of Acts has come to a close. But it hasn't come to a close. Those twenty-eight chapters were written about the Early Church.

"We are the Latter Church," Dad continued. "And until the age of grace is over, the Church Age will still be in place. The things recorded in the Book of Acts happened with the Early Church. But Christians since then have been, in effect, continuing to write that Book."

The Holy Spirit is alive and well today! He has not retired or lost any of His strength! In modern Church history, just a few generations before us, we've seen the Azusa Street Revival of the early 1900s, the Healing Revival of the '40s and '50s, and the Charismatic Renewal of the '60s and '70s. And, since then, we've seen what some call the Faith Movement of the '70s and '80s and the Holy Ghost Movement, with supernatural manifestations of joy, which began in the 1990s. Each wave brought different types of manifestations, yet they were all wrought by the power of God.

But I believe that a revival of the greater glory will incorporate *in one mighty revival* all the revivals from the beginning of the twentieth century to the present!

It's interesting that most of the pioneers of the healing and charismatic revivals have gone on to their reward. I was just a kid when the great Healing Revival began in 1947. But I remember my dad telling me that before that revival began, it seemed that many of the "old-timers"—pioneers of the faith whom God used to bring moves of God to the forefront—were going home to Glory.

That older generation had thrilled to the memories of the glory days of the '20s and '30s. But the younger ones longed for the move of God in *their* day. They hungered deeply for the miracles and signs and wonders witnessed by their predecessors. Sure, these younger ministers had seen glimpses of the glory here and there, just as we have, but their experiences paled in comparison to the experiences of past generations.

As I said, the younger ministers (my dad was one of them) yearned for a move of the Spirit and found themselves fasting, praying, and seeking God earnestly for such a move. Many a night, Dad would stay up all night praying before the Lord. He never asked God to use him specifically. He just wanted to see God move by His Spirit as He desired to move.

I remember that for much of the fall season one year, my father shut himself up in the church in Van, Texas, where he was pastoring at the time, to fast and pray for a move of God. He prayed hours on end, coming out to shower, shave, eat a little, and take care of the necessary tasks of the home and our family and of the church.

When the church service ended on Sunday nights, Mom and my sister and I would go home to our parsonage, which was right next door, and Dad would stay in the church and pray and fast. He did the same thing on Wednesday nights after the service. He did that for many weeks, week on end.

Of course, Dad wasn't the only one who was praying and seeking the Lord for a move of the Spirit. There were many others who had set themselves to seek the face of God, and truly I believe that all the prayers of those dear men and women of God in the '30s and '40s brought forth the modern revivals that are so fresh in our minds and memories today.

We of this present generation are in that same position today. We know there's more of God's Spirit that we haven't witnessed—more of Him that we've yet to experience. And because we sense what God wants to do, let us set ourselves to seek His face until the greater glory is manifested and the will of God comes to pass in the earth.

Chapter 4

TAKING THE TORCH
Following in the Footsteps of a Chosen Generation

God's glory and Presence have manifested in the lives of humankind throughout the ages. We can study it in the pages of the Bible and throughout history. Even moves of God's Spirit in the twentieth century have been recorded, such as the Azusa Street Revival, the Healing Revival, and the Charismatic Renewal. And as mentioned in the last chapter, there have been "immediate" revivals, such as what some call the Faith Movement. I believe the Faith Movement grew out of the Charismatic Renewal in which there was a renewed emphasis on teaching and on faith in God's Word.

Most recently, beginning in the 1990s, there has been a move of God's Spirit that brought renewed emphasis to manifestations of the Holy Spirit. And with that move of God came a renewed interest in and hunger for more of these manifestations of His glory. (Of course, we know that the greatest manifestation of God's glory toward man was in the Person of Christ—His birth, life, ministry, death, and resurrection.)

Your Place in God's Plan

I want to share briefly about these revivals of the past and about some of the great defenders of the faith from the beginning of Christianity. Doing so will give us some perspective and help us see our place in the scheme of things so we can take the torch that's been passed to us from generations gone by and can carry that torch, fulfilling God's plan on the earth for this generation.

Many believers are asking the question, "Where do I fit in? What is my place in God's plan?"

While I don't have specific answers for every individual, I can tell you most assuredly that *you are not here by chance*! From the very beginning, God has had a plan for the ages, and He has a place for you within the framework of that plan. Each of us must simply step up and avail ourselves, doing what we know to do where we're at right now.

In encouraging Queen Esther to step up and fulfill her call and destiny, Mordecai said to her, ". . . who knoweth whether thou art come to the kingdom for such a time as this?" (Esther 4:14 *KJV*). I believe that, whatever your place or position, you are in the Kingdom of God "for such a time as this"—for a move of God's Spirit in this day and hour!

A *Move* of God Begins With the *People* of God

My father was one of the pioneers God used to bring the faith message to his generation. In 1950, God told him, "Go teach My people faith. I've taught you faith through My Word. I permitted you to go through certain experiences, and you've learned faith both through My Word and by experience. Now go teach My people what I've taught you."

And my father did just that. Before then, it seemed as if Christians got their prayers answered, it was happenstance. But that began to change when people began to learn they could have faith in the Word and obtain the promises of God every time.

Then, later, after the time of the Charismatic Renewal, it seemed the message of faith in God's Word became prominent once again, and believers of that generation learned anew how to stand strong on the Word.

Now, two or three generations down the line from the time God spoke to my father, I think many have lost some of their zeal for the Word and for the message of faith. To many of our young people today, that message is only head knowledge. It's not revelation knowledge; it's not real to their heart or spirit.

Many others who once held dear that message of faith— and it changed their lives—have grown cold toward the Word of God. Some of them got hold of the truth many years ago and walked away from dead churches, where they practiced dry religion, to follow the Spirit of God into a deeper knowledge of God and His Word. Some even turned their backs on family traditions and friends so they could walk more deeply in the ways of the Spirit.

But revelation knowledge does not remain revelation knowledge just because you heard the message once or because you *used* to walk by faith. The truth has to stay fresh in your heart and mind, and it has to be a way of life if you are to live and prosper by it. And it has to be taught to each new generation. It has to be taught with boldness and with conviction. Otherwise, it will be dead and dry to that generation, and it will never become revelation knowledge to them.

Enough time has passed since the beginning of the Charismatic Renewal that some people refer to those days as "the good old days." This is an indictment against our generation that the glory of God is not being manifested in our midst as it once was.

Thank God for how things used to be when this move of God was at its height. Those who pioneered this move of the Spirit did their part. They sought and hungered after a move of God—not just that they would be used—but that God would display His glory in the earth that people's lives would be changed and blessed. But as good as things used to be, we should be talking more about the manifestation of God's glory—His greater glory—in *our* day.

Just as the former glory that the Bible speaks of was great, there has to be a latter glory that is greater than what once was. God Himself said, " *'The glory of this present house will be greater than the glory of the former house,' says the Lord Almighty. 'And in this place I will grant peace,' declares the Lord Almighty"* (Hag. 2:9).

Knowledge Versus Experience

From the beginning, God has desired and ordained that one generation pass on their knowledge of God to the next generation. It is no different today. We are to take the torch from generations past and keep it ablaze with the knowledge and power of God so that the move of God and the things of the Spirit will not be lost to future generations.

It seems, however, that with each passing generation, the new generation loses a little bit of what their fathers before them experienced. In other words, they're not experiencing the things that those before them experienced. They *know* about it; but it's not a present-day, living reality to them.

I thank God for my father, who was faithful to blaze a trail before me and before others so that a great move of God would not be lost to us. He did his part in passing the torch to those of us in the next generation. Now it's up to us to take that torch. We can pick up where my father and others like him left off, or we can ignore history and neglect the things of the Spirit—to the great detriment of our future.

For myself, concerning Kenneth Hagin Ministries, I intend to build on the foundation that my father laid. I am going to continue in his footsteps, staying true to the Word of God and to the will of God for this ministry. I will preach the uncompromising Word of Truth, and I will not allow it to become "watered down." People will hear the Gospel going forth from this ministry. They'll hear the message of faith being taught. I intend to have a torch, ablaze with the fires of the Spirit, to pass on to future generations!

A Walk Through History

I want to take you on a walk through the pages of church history. History tells us that the period from the time Malachi, the last book of the Old Testament, was written to the time Matthew was written was a period in which there was virtually no communication from God to man. People, even priests of God, had become lawless. They desecrated the house of the God, the Temple of God, and irreverence became the norm.

When Jesus came on the scene, born into the earth to a virgin, it was in fulfillment of God's plan. Though the world didn't exactly welcome Him with open arms, His appearing was planned, destined, and wrought by the Spirit of Almighty God.

Then upon Jesus' death, burial, resurrection, and ascension on High, men and women of the faith took the torch that Jesus had passed to His followers. Polycarp, for example, was a protégé of the Apostle John. He was one of John's personal disciples who became the Bishop of Smyrna, an ancient city in Turkey, and was later martyred for his strong Christian faith.[1]

Polycarp passed the torch to Irenaeus, whom he discipled, and others of that generation. Irenaeus, Justin Martyr, and others contended for the faith in their generation, having participated in the divine flow of God's grace.

In the third century, Early Church fathers Origen, Clement of Alexandria, and others also took their places in God's great plan to propagate the message of His saving grace through Jesus Christ.

In the fourth century, Ambrose, Augustine, and Jerome became prominent figures in Church History and had a great impact on their peers and on future generations because of the truth of God which they held so dear.

On through the Dark Ages, a remnant of brave Christian heroes held on to the truth they'd learned until the Reformation in the sixteenth century, at which time Martin Luther lifted high to his generation the blood-stained banner of the Lord Jesus Christ.

All these men were obedient to take their places in God's plan to pass on their knowledge of God to future generations so that the fires of the Holy Spirit would not be extinguished.[2]

In the 1700s, Oxford-trained scholar John Wesley preached the unadulterated Gospel of the Lord Jesus Christ. Because of his views, during the early years of his ministry, Wesley often was not allowed to preach in churches.

That's why Wesley once preached on his father's tombstone—he was not allowed to preach in the church! (At a time when so many practiced a legalistic form of worship, Wesley clung boldly to the simple but powerful message of the Gospel.) Most graveyards then were on church property. So John Wesley went outside the church, stood on his father's grave, and preached! He couldn't be kicked off his own father's tombstone!

Throughout the pages of history, there have always been people willing to step out of their comfort zone and out of the status quo to carry the torch of God to future generations.

Moving from the 1800s and into the early-to-mid-1900s, men and women of God such as F.F. Bosworth, Maria Woodworth-Etter, John G. Lake, Aimee Semple McPherson, Charles Parham, Charles Price, Smith Wigglesworth, and many others, continued to carry the torch of faith.

Gordon Lindsay, who knew John G. Lake personally, testified to my father that in one five-year period in Lake's ministry, more than 100,000 healings were documented. Lake was known as the modern-day apostle of faith to Africa.

My dad was saved at the age of 15 while on his deathbed and later received healing of a deformed heart and incurable blood disease by acting on Mark 11:23 and 24 for himself. Afterward, he entered the ministry, and his ministry was influenced by some of these men and women of faith of the previous generation.

I was born in 1939, and as early as 1943 and 1944, I can remember instances in connection with the move of God's Spirit in Dad's meetings. He was pastoring a little church in Farmersville, Texas, which at the time, wasn't as big as some church *platforms* today!

Every Saturday night, Dad preached on the subject of healing. And more and more people began attending those healing meetings. The war was on, and it seemed that people in that small farming community (which, incidentally, was home to WWII decorated soldier Audie Murphy) came into town from all directions on Saturdays.

There was no air-conditioning in that little church. They just opened the windows and held healing services. Many times, there were as many people outside as there were inside who came to hear Dad preach and teach on faith and healing. And as he ministered, the power of God was demonstrated.

In February 1949, my father completed his work as pastor of the church in Van, Texas, and that was the last church he ever pastored. He began his traveling ministry, which evolved into the ministry you can see today based and spread over 100 acres in Broken Arrow, Oklahoma!

At about the same time dad began his travels, out of the hills of Oklahoma came a young man of native American descent. His long legs strode across many a platform as he preached messages, such as "The Fourth Man in the Fire" and "Turn Your Faith Loose!" With a heart full of fervency, he'd always sing the song, "When He Reached Down His Hand for Me."

I was present in many of Oral Roberts' services, and I have vivid memories of those evangelistic meetings in which countless lives were changed by the glory of God. In my mind's eye, I can still see and hear Brother Roberts as if it were just yesterday.

Then in the mid 1950s, although no one had done it before that we know of, a couple named T.L. and Daisy Osborn went to the nations, renting soccer stadiums and filling them with crowds of people who came to hear the Gospel preached. Others said it couldn't be done, but they did it successfully, and signs and wonders were wrought on behalf of thousands by the power of the Spirit.

But none of these exploits could ever have been accomplished had not men and women afire with the flames of the Spirit in their heart "carried the torch" in their time. When you are willing and obedient to carry the torch of the glory of God, there is no such thing as the word *impossible*!

Right in the middle of this tremendous move of the Spirit in the mid-1950s was a man by the name of Kenneth Hagin, my namesake. Because of his great love for God and for people, I truly believe my father was one of the greatest men to walk the face of this earth. I would not trade my godly heritage for anything.

Dad never had a tent or went to the large auditoriums to hold meetings, because the Lord told him to go to the churches. He'd go to various churches and hold meetings that lasted up to eight weeks or longer. He took his time and taught the people so they could learn how to receive from a giving God with the hand of faith.

There were countless others who took part in this great revival of the '50s. They are the precious men and women of God who passed the torch to our generation.

From Glory to Glory: An Awakened Generation

As the Healing Revival gave way to the Charismatic Renewal, the Full Gospel Businessmen's Association began, headed by Demos Shakarian. Many of us (or our parents or grandparents) came out of that movement. The Charismatic Renewal was a time of great outpouring, and I think that among others, two of the greatest leaders and proponents of that movement were my own father and John Osteen.

Let me quote to you an excerpt from John Osteen's book *This Awakening Generation* that was written during the emergence of the Charismatic Renewal:

> Like a sleeping giant rousing itself out of a deep sleep, the true Church, which is the Body of Christ, is awakening.
>
> The prophet Joel said, "It shall come to pass in the last days," saith God, "I shall pour out My Spirit on all flesh" [Acts 2:17 *KJV*]. This prophecy is being fulfilled today.
>
> Ministers and members of all the historic denominations are receiving the baptism in the Holy Ghost. They are speaking in other tongues, praying for the sick, casting out devils, seeing miracles and experiencing the mighty gifts of the Spirit as recorded in First Corinthians, Chapter 12, and demonstrated in the Book of Acts. . . .
>
> With tear-stained faces these awakened people are climbing the hill of God to get above the fog and smog of tradition and sectarianism. They want God and the power of His Holy Spirit.
>
> They want more than religion. They want the miracle life of the Lord Jesus Christ that comes through the mighty baptism in the Holy Ghost. . . .
>
> They want God's supernatural, miracle working power that will enable them to effectively reach the lost, doomed and dying before it is everlastingly too late.[3]

The Charismatic Renewal arose from a desire to break away from dead, dry, manmade religion and to worship the true and living God. But I think we as Charismatics have become so accustomed to our ways of doing things that we have our own "fog and smog of tradition." *It's time to wake up!*

It's time that we, with our tear-stained faces, climb the hill of God and rise above the fog and smog of our own traditions. We need to take up and carry the torch of the true move of the Spirit of God.

Again, the fire of the Holy Spirit needs to burn brightly in our lives, and the message of faith in God needs to be preached stronger than ever before. In the 1980s, that message was fresh and strong, and it was preached without apology or compromise. Churches grew robust and became deeply established on the truths that were taught.

'Memory Lane' or New Manifestations of Glory?

But now that we've rolled into a new millennium, we need to realize that it's our time! We can't live on the revivals of yesteryear. If we simply continue living on "Memory Lane" with only the embers of past memories burning dimly, we will die in the smoke. But I believe that this will be a generation that will fan those embers into a brightly shining flame, and will hold forth that torch of the glory and power of God to an awakening generation today!

I want to put in perspective for you the time in which we are living today. I want you to see that we are living in an exciting time in history! Will we be a generation that's going to just "play church" and be content with business as usual? Will we be satisfied with the commonplace? Or will we take our places as men and women of destiny who are ". . . come to the kingdom for such a time as this" (Esther 4:14 *KJV*)?

A Return to Virtue

I think it's time that the Church as a whole began to focus on Christian values. And I believe it needs to be emphasized from church pulpits. As my father often said, people will rise to the level of what they are taught. For example, if you preach on love, they will grow and rise to the level of walking in love.

A few years ago, a *U.S. News and World Report* survey said, in effect, forty-three percent of Americans say there is no one set of values we should adhere to. I suspect that those numbers have risen today.

But I want to tell you something. There *is* a set of values— *one* set of values—and it is found in the pages of God's Word! We hear so much talk about America's need to change. But it's not going to change until we as believers pick up the torch, preach those values, and then live what we preach.

The Church has reached a point where we've soft-pedaled sin, so to speak, and it has become all right in the eyes of many in the faith to do things that are worldly and unseemly. Those things clearly go cross-grain to the Word of God, but the message has been lost in many pulpits, and many Christians no longer have a clear value system.

There are so many today who are oppressed, bruised, and downtrodden. Their lives have lost meaning; they wander through life directionless, without a set of values to live by and without help and hope. But the reason we are here on this earth as believers is to set free those who are down and out! This is our time! Will we do something about it, or will we continue to shake our heads and only talk about the worsening condition of the world around us?

Look at Jesus' own words in Luke 4:18.

LUKE 4:18 (KJV)

18 The Spirit of the Lord is upon me, because he hath anointed me to preach the gospel to the poor; he hath sent me to heal the brokenhearted, to preach deliverance to the captives, and recovering of sight to the blind, to set at liberty them that are bruised.

Friend, *we* as believers have been anointed and appointed to do the works of Jesus on the earth (John 14:12). And it's time we did it! We are to walk this land, setting free the captive and liberating those who've been bruised and downtrodden. This is our time!

Quitting Is Not an Option!

In 1957, I ran track in the state of Oregon at Canyonville Bible Academy. That year, my team and I ran in the 880 relay at the state meet in Eugene (as a matter of fact, it was on May 18, 1957, at nine o'clock in the evening).

I took my position on the backstretch to run my 220 yards. I stood there, poised and ready to run, waiting for my teammate to hand off the baton to me. We had been a fast team all year and worked well together. As a rule, about the time my teammate would hand me the baton, he'd yell, "Go!" and I'd take off! I'd already be running by the time he slapped that baton into my hand!

That particular night, I kept looking and listening for my teammate. But it was dark on the backstretch, and I couldn't see clearly. I kept thinking, *He should have been here by now*. At one point, I turned around, and, suddenly, I could see his face in the darkness. His teeth were clenched tightly, and every muscle in his face was strained. He was working so hard that he couldn't even speak, much less yell. But I saw him motion to me, and—*pop*—that baton hit my hand just in time; I was off and running.

Two hundred and ten yards later, I was feeling his pain! Just 10 yards before I reached our next teammate, I began to see white spots in front of my eyes. My body was screaming, *Just quit! It's too hard!*

But I wouldn't even slow down. Then, as I passed that baton to my teammate, I took two more steps and fell flat on my face in the grass.

I related that account to illustrate the point that once we decide to take up the torch that has been passed to us, there should be no turning back. We should have the same determination to obey God as I did to win that race. We can't use the excuse, "It's just so hard. I don't know whether I can go on."

Friend, Jesus paid a big price to lay a firm foundation for all of us. But if we decide not to build on that foundation, we will be held accountable.

So quitting is not an option! Men and women of God who went before us have done their part. They were faithful to carry the torch. And now it's our time! Let's hold on to the teaching we've heard. Let's remember the consecration and dedication of our forefathers. Let's hold fast to the move of the

Spirit that we have been privileged to witness. And let's carry the torch to our generation and to the *next* generation.

No, I'm not saying the road will always be easy. In fact, the road to success is not always straight and smooth. But I challenge you to take your place and be willing to march ahead into the unknown—if need be, with nothing underneath you but the Word of God. God will light your path and make your way plain, but you have to be willing! And you have to be obedient when He says, "Go!"

One pastor said to me, "I hear what you're saying, but if I do what you're saying, I might lose people from my church."

I told him, "If you preach what you believe according to God's Word, and people leave because they don't like it, it shouldn't affect you. You just keep on doing what God is telling you to do, and He will send people to your church who are hungry for the Word of God and for a true move of His Spirit.

"Besides," I continued, "people who scowl and scoff at the moving of the Spirit are like wet blankets: they will put out what fire you do have in your church!"

Those aren't the kind of people you need supporting you. You need those who will keep the flames of the Spirit fanned and burning brightly!

My father and so many of his contemporaries demonstrated great love and great faith in their lives and ministries. And demonstrations of the Spirit were wrought through them. But now it is our time! What will we do with the lessons we've learned and with the examples that have been set before us?

Many of us have been playing church way too long. We've been content just to experience God's Spirit inside the four walls of our churches. But the greater glory is not just for us inside the walls of our local churches. That glory is for the *world*!

There are signs that hang over the exit doorways of our church auditorium that read, "The worship is over—now the service begins." Your pastor alone can't take the Gospel to the four corners of the earth. But *each one of us can* by starting right where we are.

As I said before, seeing the greater glory of God starts in our own hearts. We have to be more hungry for a move of God than we are to better ourselves or to pursue our own dreams and goals. And we have to be *willing*—willing to take the torch that's been passed and to follow in the faithful footsteps of the generation before us.

---

[1] Henry H. Halley, *Halley's Bible Handbook*, 24th ed. (Grand Rapids, Mich.: Regency Reference Library, 1965), 749.

[2] Tim Dowley, ed., *The History of Christianity*, rev. ed. (Batavia, Ill.: Lion Publishing Corp., 1990), 94,100,107,119,149,196–197,206–208,368–369.

[3] John Osteen, *This Awakening Generation* (Houston: John Osteen Ministries, 1964), 7,10–11. Used by permission.

Chapter 5

THE DIVINE MIX OF FAITH AND THE SPIRIT

There's more to preparing for a great move of God than just *wanting* to experience His glory. There is a divine cooperation that must take place if we are to enter in to all that God has for us. You've probably heard it said, "If you want to receive from God, find out how He works and work with Him." It's true. If we really want the full measure of God's blessings, we're going to have to receive it *His* way. ✓

You've also probably heard the saying, "Faith is the language of Heaven." The Bible says that the just shall live by faith (Rom. 1:17; Gal. 3:11; Heb. 10:38), and without faith, it is impossible to please Him [God] (Heb. 11:6). In this chapter, I'm going to show the connection between faith and the greater glory, or the divine mix of faith and the Spirit.

Obedience: An Act of Faith and Cooperation

Lynette and I have been married nearly 40 years. In the early days of our marriage, I earned $50 per week as a full-time associate pastor. Lynette had gone to school to be a hair stylist, and had it not been for her income as a stylist during the first five years of our ministry we probably wouldn't have made it financially. After that time, she never worked again as a hair stylist.

Then later, in the mid-'70s, after we joined with my dad to get RHEMA Bible Training Center started, Lynette began putting in many hours at the ministry without taking a salary. She didn't begin receiving a salary for five or six years after we began working with Kenneth Hagin Ministries.

Now, I'm not saying this because we think that all of our hard work has somehow entitled us to the blessings of God, or because I'm trying to justify the blessings that we enjoy today. I'm telling you this to illustrate the principle of obedience and faithfulness that opens the way for God to bless you. There is a definite connection between your obeying God and your receiving more of His glory. (I will cover the subject of obedience more in-depth in another chapter.)

Someone asked, "Well, I thought that all I needed was *faith* to receive from God?"

Yes, but if you have faith—if you believe God is who He says He is—you will do what He says to do in your life, and that entails obedience and faithfulness! For example, if God tells you to give, you will obey and give because you believe that God is who He says He is and that He will do what He says He will do. And as a result of your faith, you will believe that God will make grace abound to you (2 Cor. 9:8), that He will meet your need (Phil. 4:19), and that you will reap a harvest of return from your obedience in giving (2 Cor. 9:6–11).

Lynette and I have continually sown money into people and ministries. It has been a way of life for us. But I remember one incident in particular in the very early days of our ministry when God spoke to us to give a certain amount, and, in the natural, we really couldn't afford to give it. We had prayed and agreed together, asking the Lord to show us what we should give. Afterward, I said to Lynette, "What do you think?"

She answered, "I believe the Lord wants us to give such-and-such amount," and she named the amount.

I said, "That's the exact figure God spoke to my heart."

As I said, in the natural, it was a sacrifice for us to give that much money. But we knew God was telling us to do it, so we did it.

Just a few months later, I received a telephone call from my dad. "Son, how would you like to have a new car?" he asked.

I didn't even have to think about it. I responded, "Well, the one we have barely runs." It was an older car, and we were always having problems with it.

"Well," he said, "a woman just approached me about buying you a brand-new one. She said that as she was praying, the Lord told her, 'Buy Brother Hagin's son a new car.'"

Now, this woman didn't know me. We met her later when we received the car. In fact, at the time the Lord spoke to her, she didn't even know Brother Hagin had a son. After the

Lord had spoken to her, she was in one of Dad's meetings, and afterward, she asked him, "Brother Hagin, do you have a son?"

"Yes," he replied, "he's the associate pastor over at such-and-such church," and he named the church.

She then related to Dad what the Lord had said to her. "Tell him," she said, "to go down to the dealership and pick out whatever kind of car he wants."

We chose a brand-new Delta 88 Oldsmobile. That was 1969, and, incidentally, we've never been without a new car since.

We immediately recognized the blessing of that new car as something that God did for us because we had obeyed Him in finances just a few months earlier. I know I never would have received that new car if we hadn't done what God told us to do in giving that offering.

You've probably heard or read of some of the accounts of my dad's obedience, including obedience in finances, that opened the way for God to bless and use him.

Once, during Depression Days, the Lord spoke to him to give a young evangelist and his family $10 at Christmastime. That was twice the amount of a usual offering, and in those days, a man could support a family of five for less than $40 a month! So that was a big offering back then, but my dad did it. It was about a week's pay for my dad, and he hadn't even bought my mom's Christmas present. Later, he found out that the young man was penniless and had nothing for Christmas for his kids or for Christmas dinner.

Sometime later, Dad had another chance to obey God in finances. (Now, I'm not saying that he never gave unless the Lord spoke to him. I'm saying that these were instances in which God specifically spoke to him, and each time, the amount was more than he thought he could afford to give in the natural.)

One Sunday evening just before service was about to begin, a fellow minister got off a bus in front of Dad's church (the church was right on the highway which went through our town). Dad greeted him and asked him if he would take the service and minister to the people.

The man agreed, and while he was preaching, the Lord told Dad specifically to give the man $12.50 out of his own pocket. That was more than a week's salary for my dad, but again, he obeyed God.

Then two years later, Dad was called on to minister to a woman on her deathbed. She was in the last stages of an incurable disease. Doctors said she would be dead in just a few days.

As Dad and Mom knelt beside the woman's bed to pray, the Lord told Dad, "Don't pray. Stand up and say to her, 'The Lord told me to tell you you're healed. Get up.'"

She did, and God did—the woman was made completely well! The following Sunday, she was in church shouting the victory!

After Dad ministered to that woman and she received her healing, the Lord spoke to Dad again as he was on the way home. He said, "I couldn't have used you today if you hadn't obeyed Me on that $10 and that $12.50."

You see, the inward voice of the Spirit that told Dad to give that money was the same voice that told him what to say to that woman to cause her to be completely healed. If you won't hear and obey God in one area—in the giving of an offering, for example—He can't count on you to hear and obey Him when He asks you to step out so that He can use you to bring about healing or some other blessing for someone else.

If God can't use you in one area, He very likely won't use you in some other area, either. The Bible says if you're faithful over a few things, God can trust you with many things (*see* Matt. 25:21, 23).

There are two principles at work here that I want you to see—that of obedience and faithfulness to God in everything, and that of learning to hear His voice. Both entail a cooperation with Him. As I said, if we want to receive from God, we're going to have to find out how God works and then work with Him.

God desires to move in our midst. But, as I said, it's not all up to Him; it's up to us whether we will cooperate with Him so that He can do what He wants to do in the earth through us. Will we be obedient when He calls on us to use us in some way? Will we be faithful and stay with what He's calling us to do even when the going gets tough? I believe we will!

There is no end to the great things we will witness when God manifests His greater glory on the earth. I believe it will be spectacular beyond anything we've seen before. The Holy Spirit can do in a matter of seconds what might take us weeks, months, or even years to do on our own. And He can make even the impossible *possible*.

The Spirit and the Word Agree

The reason I'm talking about the divine mix of faith and the Spirit is because a move of the Holy Spirit in your life doesn't negate your need to walk by faith. And the opposite is also true: Your walking by faith doesn't negate your need for a move of the Spirit in your life. The Spirit and the Word work together.

For example, in Matthew chapter 12, Jesus talks about what happens when an evil spirit is cast out of a man, and the man doesn't do what he's supposed to do after God has delivered him.

MATTHEW 12:43–45

43 "When an evil spirit comes out of a man, it goes through arid places seeking rest and does not find it.

44 Then it says, 'I will return to the house I left.' When it arrives, it finds the house unoccupied, swept clean and put in order.

45 Then it goes and takes with it seven other spirits more wicked than itself, and they go in and live there. And the final condition of that man is worse than the first . . . ."

When the Spirit of God moves in your life, it's up to you to maintain what He has done for you. You have to *keep* what God gives! In other words, a person could be healed by a spectacular move of the Spirit. But if that person doesn't understand healing from the Word of God and doesn't stand his ground, the enemy may steal his healing. The enemy will try to bring back the same old symptoms, and the person will just side in with the circumstances and say, "Well, I guess I didn't get healed after all."

So, you see, just because the Spirit of God moves in a powerful way, that does not do away with your need to be full of the Word of God. In a previous chapter, I talked about the Charismatic Renewal in which teaching and the Word of God were greatly emphasized.

We *still* need a strong emphasis on teaching and the Word!

Just because God is doing something new in the earth doesn't negate what He's done in the past. We need it *all*—we need to experience and walk in *everything* that God has done and is doing, not just part of it.

God's Glory in the Fires of Affliction

I can't stress enough the importance of faith in our seeing greater and greater manifestations of God's glory. As I said, a move of God's Spirit doesn't do away with our need for strong faith in God's Word. In the Gospels, we see Jesus saying to Martha, the sister of Lazarus, whom Jesus raised from the dead, "'. . . Did I not tell you that if you believed, you would see the glory of God?'" (John 11:40).

When the pressures of life press hard against us, will we stay true to God? Will we believe Him and see His glory manifested in our situation? When the enemy tries to attack us, the first thing out of our mouth should be the Word of God. That can only happen if we're continually abiding in the Word. John 15:7 says, "If you remain in me [Jesus] and my words remain in you, ask whatever you wish, and it will be given you."

There are many who are in Christ, all right; they are abiding, or remaining, in Him. But His Word is not abiding in them. That's why they don't get their prayers answered. They can't ask what they wish and have it be done for them—because they're not fulfilling the first part of that verse: The Word is not abiding in them, in their heart.

In a crisis, you can always tell whether or not believers have been abiding in the Word. You can tell by the words of their mouth. If they don't have the Word in them, when pressure comes, they'll say something such as, "Oh, God, what are we going to do?"

I thank God for the home I grew up in, because amidst the tests and pressures of life that we faced, I learned from my dad's example what it meant to have steadfast faith. When I was about eight or nine years old, Dad began traveling in field ministry and was gone most of the time. My mother stayed home and raised my sister and me, and we sometimes traveled with Dad as a family during the summer when we were out of school.

My mom, sister, and I had $25 a week that we lived on, and that's the amount we had to spend to buy whatever it was we needed—food, toiletries, clothes, shoes, and so forth. At times, when Dad was home, my mother would say something to him about finances—about something we needed or a crisis we were facing. Dad would always say, "This is just another opportunity to prove that God's Word works."

In my mind's eye, I can still see him sitting at our kitchen table, just as calm as calm can be, no matter what it was that we were facing. Then he would begin quoting Scripture. He never wavered in his faith, and God always came through for us.

Many times, Dad would write and tell us (we didn't have money for long-distance phone calls back then), "At 3:00 on Sunday afternoon, I will be in the church between services. I'll have my Bible open to Mark 11:23. You agree with me for the Sunday night offering."

Sometimes Dad would be in a different time zone, so we would calculate the time we needed to get together and agree in prayer with him. You see, there's no distance in the Spirit. Though Dad was ministering in another state and we were at home, we could agree together and count it as done by faith. We experienced some tremendous answers to prayer as a result. But we never would have seen the hand of God move on our behalf if we hadn't stayed with the Word in the hard times.

I experienced some hard times of my own growing up without a father at home for long periods at a time. The first fight I ever got into in my life was because a kid at school ridiculed me over the fact that my dad traveled and was gone so much. He said to me, "Your dad ain't never home. He's just running around . . ."

That's as far as he got before I busted him. No, I shouldn't have hit him, and I'm not proud of the fact that I did it. At the time, I didn't know how not to let those kinds of things get to me. I did learn, though, and God was able to establish me to the point that when people said bad things about me, I would just dig my heels into the ground, so to speak, and refuse to move off the Word of God that I was trusting in.

I still deal with people saying things about me, my dad, and the ministry that are unkind and untrue. I could let it get to me to this day and take the attitude, "That hurts. Poor me. Listen to what they're saying about me. Isn't it sad?"

But if I did that, I would have to take a step back spiritually. I know I can't stand on the Word and at the same time take offense at someone else's actions.

I know other traveling ministers can relate to this—there have been times I've traveled somewhere to minister, and afterward, the pastor just shook my hand and said, "God bless you, Brother." I would have to find my own place to stay during the meeting and buy my own meals if I had the money. If I didn't have money, I did without. After I fulfilled my obligation to preach, I'd get in my car and begin driving home saying, "Thank You, Lord, for Your Word."

Stick With the Word, and the Word Will Stick With You!

Thank God, the Word of God never changes, and that Word can be depended on, no matter what the situation or circumstances! I learned that attitude of faith from my father. That's the attitude you're going to have to have if you're going to stay with the Word and experience God's blessings and His glory.

The devil will try to bring people and circumstances your way to get you to move off the Word. He will bring thoughts and images of the past to try to bring up old hurts. But in those times, you have to dig in and refuse to quit believing God. You have to say, "Hallelujah! I am more than a conqueror in Christ Jesus [Rom. 8:37]. No weapon formed against me will prosper [Isa. 54:17]. If God be for me, who can be against me? [Rom. 8:31]."

As you do that, you'll begin to feel buoyed up on the inside, in your spirit, and those tempting thoughts will begin to fade from memory if you will not quit.

The Attitude of Faith

I want to talk a little more about this attitude of faith. Second Corinthians 4:13 says, "We having the same spirit of faith, according as it is written, I believed, and therefore have I spoken; we also believe, and therefore speak" (*KJV*). One paraphrase says, "We have the same *attitude* of faith . . ." (*The Heart of Paul, A Relational Paraphrase of the New Testament* by Ben Campbell Johnson).

Having the spirit or attitude of faith causes you to operate in faith as a matter of course: You believe and, therefore, speak. It is not a mechanical function of mere head knowledge, but a spiritual operation of the heart. It is God's Word coming out of your spirit to produce something that did not exist before.

When the Word penetrates your heart to such an extent that it affects your believing and your saying, you are operating in that spirit or attitude of faith. I like to say it like this: It's an attitude of the heart expressed with the mouth. It's an attitude that believes God's Word and speaks what it believes!

Many people are quick to say, "Yes, I have that same spirit of faith." It's easy to say that in the absence of tests or trials when everything is going smoothly around you. But let's look at the context in which the Apostle Paul wrote this verse.

2 CORINTHIANS 4:8–13 (KJV)

8 We are troubled on every side, yet not distressed; we are perplexed, but not in despair;

9 Persecuted, but not forsaken; cast down, but not destroyed;

10 Always bearing about in the body the dying of the Lord Jesus, that the life also of Jesus might be made manifest in our body.

11 For we which live are alway delivered unto death for Jesus' sake, that the life also of Jesus might be made manifest in our mortal flesh.

12 So then death worketh in us, but life in you.

13 WE HAVING THE SAME SPIRIT OF FAITH, according as it is written, I believed, and therefore have I spoken; we also believe, and therefore speak

What was Paul talking about in verses 8 and 9 when he said he had been troubled, perplexed, persecuted, and cast down? We have some clue as we study this Epistle that Paul wrote to the Church at Corinth. In chapter 11, Paul talks about his ". . . labours more abundant . . . stripes above measure . . . prisons more frequent [and] . . . deaths oft" (v. 23 *KJV*).

The following verses give us more detail.

2 CORINTHIANS 11:24–28 (KJV)

24 Of the Jews five times received I forty stripes save one.

25 Thrice was I beaten with rods, once was I stoned, thrice I suffered shipwreck, a night and a day I have been in the deep;

26 In journeyings often, in perils of waters, in perils of robbers, in perils by mine own countrymen, in perils by the heathen, in perils in the city, in perils in the wilderness, in perils in the sea, in perils among false brethren;

27 In weariness and painfulness, in watchings often, in hunger and thirst, in fastings often, in cold and nakedness.

28 Beside those things that are without, that which cometh upon me daily, the care of all the churches.

In the Old Testament, the Psalmist David said, "I believed, therefore have I spoken: I was greatly afflicted" (Ps. 116:10 *KJV*). David spoke out the fact that he was in trouble, but he also spoke his faith in God, just as Paul did. In midst of pain and affliction, David was saying, "I kept my faith."

In the midst of pain and affliction, you can either keep your faith and talk about the Word and about God's faithfulness, or you can focus on the circumstances. You can have an attitude of faith and allow God to bring you out of your test or trial, or you can have an attitude of failure and fear that will cause you to throw up your hands in desperation and quit. And the path you take—the path of faith or the path of fear, doubt, and unbelief—will largely be determined by what's in your heart and by what comes out of your mouth!

Luke 6:45 says, "A good man out of the good treasure of his heart bringeth forth that which is good; and an evil man out of the evil treasure of his heart bringeth forth that which is evil: for OF THE ABUNDANCE OF THE HEART HIS MOUTH SPEAKETH" (*KJV*). I like the *Twentieth Century New Testament* translation, which says, ". . . for what fills a man's heart will rise to his lips."

In the midst of your pain and deep hurt, it's what you have in you in abundance that's going to rise to your lips. Are you abiding in God's Word? Is your heart so full of the Word that in the fires of affliction, you can maintain your faith in God? When failure seems imminent with no natural way of escape, can you shout from the depths of your being, "I always triumph in Christ Jesus [2 Cor. 2:14]! I am more than a conqueror through Him [Rom. 8:37]!"?

I challenge you to maintain an attitude of faith even in the midst of tests and trials. Remember, what fills your heart will rise to your lips. If you allow your heart to be filled with offenses and continue to dwell on the wrong that someone has committed against you, you will be held captive in the arena of defeat. But if you keep the Word of God uppermost in your heart and mind, the power of that Word will propel you out of defeat into glorious victory!

Chapter 6

THE GREAT EXCHANGE
Your Pain for His Power

As I've said before, I believe we will see great and mighty things when God manifests His greater glory on the earth. I believe it will be spectacular beyond anything we've seen before. The glory of God can accomplish in a matter of seconds what might take us weeks, months, or even years to do on our own. And when our situation is impossible, He can make the impossible *possible*!

In Scripture, we see God as a possibility God, even when the situation was impossible in the natural. Just look at the children of Israel's exodus from Egypt and how God parted the sea when they were hemmed in by mountains, enemy troops, and an ocean! That was an impossible situation, but God led His people across that sea on dry land. Our God is indeed a possibility God!

Whenever I autograph one of my books, I always write the Scripture reference Luke 18:27, in which Jesus says, ". . . The things which are impossible with men are possible with God" (*KJV*). I have lived by that verse of Scripture as

I've faced the challenges, tests, and trials of life that we all encounter at one time or another.

I've been in pulpit ministry in some capacity from the time I was about 19 years old. But I've been around the things pertaining to the ministry for as many years as I am old! When I was born, my father was pastoring a little church in Farmersville, Texas. So you *could* say I've been associated with church life and with the ministry all of my life! My family and I attended every church service Dad held in the churches he pastored. And I remember as a very young boy helping him around the church—sweeping, cleaning bathrooms, painting, hanging wallpaper, and, later, installing plumbing and electrical work.

Over the years, I've poured concrete, framed walls, and have done whatever was needed so that the work of God could go forward. I have seen what went on behind the scenes to make a ministry grow and be productive, blessing people and changing lives. I've also seen a lot of the ministry side of things, and it wasn't always rosy.

I've seen people devastated by tragedy, emotionally torn apart by the crises of life. I've seen parents suffer great agony over problems with their children, and I've seen teenagers deeply troubled by problems at home and problems with peers and the pressures of life. I've witnessed families losing everything they owned and facing financial disaster beyond imagination. I've seen marriages fall apart and embittered children lost to the world and its ways.

But I've also seen people have a real experience with God and receive His wisdom, goodness, power, and love to change their circumstances and bring healing to their lives. I've seen financial loss reversed, and I've seen families that were torn apart restored by God's limitless resources.

You Are Never Alone

The problems of life are real. Tragedy is real. Sickness, disease, and the loss of jobs and income are real. No matter what our education, strengths, skills, or financial status, every one of us at one time or another will encounter problems that lie beyond our resources to solve. We will (if we haven't already) come to the realization that we have limitations. But along with that realization, we also need to realize that there is hope beyond ourselves, a ray of light beyond the dark tunnel of our human limitations. And we need to know that we are not alone.

No doubt we've all reached times in life when we simply didn't know what to do. The circumstances seemed impossible from our standpoint. It's during those times that we can throw up our hands in despair and allow feelings of hopelessness overwhelm us. Or we can look to the Limitless One and allow Him to strengthen and revive us so that we are aware of the possibilities that exist with Him.

God Never Intended That We Try to Make It on Our Own

So what *do* you do if your marriage is in trouble? If your kids are rebelling against you and the things of God? If your doctor gives you a bad report? If you find out after putting in years at your place of employment that your job has been terminated?

I can't specifically tell you what to do in each situation and circumstance of life. But I can point you to the One who can—and who *will*! Some problems arise through no fault of our own; others we bring on ourselves. But God wants to show us the way out of *all* of them!

Certainly, in the tests and trials of life, we need to make sure there isn't something we're doing to prevent God from helping us. (For example, if we're not walking in love, we can short-circuit the power of God in our lives even though He is willing to help us.) But once we do the things we know to do, we must allow this timeless truth to permeate our heart and dominate our thinking: *What is impossible with man is possible with God.*

Your Revelation Is Your Foundation

That's what Jesus said in Luke 18:27: ". . . The things which are impossible with men are possible with God" (*KJV*). We have to receive a revelation of that truth on the inside of us. It can't be mere words we speak with our mouth that our heart doesn't agree with. It can't be mere words that we just *mentally* agree with. This truth has to become an attitude of life. Then we will be in a strong, steady position to reap those God-possibilities in our lives.

Throughout the Word of God, we find God telling people, in effect, "If you will do such-and-such, then I will do something for you." For example, in Exodus 14:13, He told His people through Moses, ". . . Fear ye not, STAND STILL, and see the salvation of the Lord, which he will shew to you to day . . ." (*KJV*). Notice the people had to do something: They had to "fear not" and to "stand still." They had to trust the Lord and believe in His delivering power.

It seems that some people would rather call just about every prayer line in the country than to simply trust God and take Him at His Word for themselves. Or they have the idea that if they can get certain ministers to pray for them, God will move *for sure* then!

So many people today don't want to do anything in the way of cooperating with God and His Word to receive His blessing. Yet they still want God to go ahead and move on their behalf. But it doesn't work that way. We have some responsibility as to whether or not we're blessed. We have a part to play if the faith walk is to be a way of life.

No Matter What—God Is Still God!

One Sunday morning several years ago as I was getting ready to deliver to my congregation the message I'd prepared, the Lord said to me, "Don't preach on that. Preach *this* . . . ," and He gave me the message entitled, "No Matter What—God Is Still God!" It was a powerful, riveting message that inspired the church and stirred them to cling to their faith in an unchanging God in the midst of turbulent, uncertain times.

As I delivered that message, I could not have known in myself what would transpire that week. On Tuesday following that Sunday morning message, one of the traveling ministers in our church passed away. He was widely known and was an anointed, gifted young man in the prime of his life and ministry, yet his life was cut short. It was a potentially devastating blow to our congregation, as well as to our RHEMA alumni and others who knew him, but that message the Lord gave me answered so many questions that would have otherwise bewildered them. They had something to stand on for support during a difficult time.

I've had occasion to preach that sermon to myself again and again over the years, including when my beloved father passed away. I have actually lived that message and that verse of Scripture, "The things which are impossible with men are possible with God" (Luke 18:27 *KJV*). When your grief seems unbearable and your loss unendurable, God is still God, and a future bright with promise is still possible with Him.

But, you see, until something becomes a revelation on the inside of you, you won't really act on it. You might go along with it mentally when you hear it. But it won't be a living reality to you, and it won't produce anything of lasting value in your life.

In your situation right now, you may think it sounds impossible that God's Word can become more real to you than whatever it is you're going through. But it *is* possible! When God's Word becomes revelation to you in your heart, it will be a rock to you that will not be shaken. Though the wind howls, the thunder rolls, and the lightning flashes, you can remain steady and calm. Nothing can take the truth of

God's Word away from you if you'll hold on to it—not circumstances, not other people, and not the enemy himself! And that Word that you hold on to will produce something powerful in your life.

Man Is Limited

Let's look more in-depth at Luke 18:27: "The things which are impossible with men are possible with God" (*KJV*). The first part of that verse says, "the things which are impossible with men." Someone might ask, "Well, isn't that a negative statement?" No, it is simply a testament to man's limitations.

Natural man is limited. He is often limited by his knowledge or intellect. He is limited by his natural strength—by his finite physical body—which the Bible says is perishing day by day (2 Cor. 4:16).

It is a natural fact that as most people age, they're not as strong as they used to be. I know for myself that I can't keep up with the younger guys on the basketball court or on the softball field now that I'm over 60! Certainly, a person can take care of himself by eating right and by exercising, and he should do those things. But he is going to age—he's going to get older if he keeps on living—no matter what.

Understanding Our Limitations Can Propel Us Forward by God's Unlimited Grace

We need to understand who we are as human beings to appreciate what God can do through and for us. We must know that in ourselves, we are nothing, and that apart from

God, we can do nothing. We need to know ourselves in our limited state. But then we must also understand that we have the unique ability as believers to live in and have access to two realms: the *limited earthly* realm and the *limitless heavenly* realm. I will talk more about that later in this chapter.

In identifying our limitations, it is important that we understand our individual strengths and weaknesses. Too many people are trying to be something they're not supposed to be—simply because they want to!

For example, there are a lot of people who are trying to be pastors who aren't called to be pastors. Maybe they should be associate pastors. That's the area to which God has called many, but, very often, they try to do something else that's beyond their grace. (I have actually counseled certain ministers along this line who have gotten angry with me for saying that!)

There's nothing wrong with functioning where God has placed you and in the area where your unique gifts and abilities can be best utilized. In fact, that is what we *should* be doing, because that's where God's blessing can come upon us in the greatest measure, and where we can be the greatest blessing to the Body of Christ and to the world.

Throughout the Bible, we see great leaders whom God used to bring deliverance, blessing, and protection to His people. We should all try to emulate their *faith*, but that doesn't mean we should try to emulate their *office*. None of these leaders fulfilled his or her assigned task without the help of others. And no leader today can accomplish what God has called him or her to do without faithful partners called of God to help carry out the vision He has given that leader.

For example, King David didn't lead his people without a cabinet of advisors, secretaries, scribes, and so forth, to help him carry out the task. And let's not forget David's mighty men of valor, who did exploits as they fulfilled the call of God up on their lives to assist the king.

Some people function very effectively with someone else's plan; they are gifted and anointed to do so. But if they had to start getting a plan on their own, they would cease to be effective.

We need to identify our gifts and talents as well as our weaknesses. If your talent lies in one area, and you're trying to function in other areas, you're going to be frustrated! Certainly, you can feel challenged when you're functioning in the middle of God's perfect will. But He gives you grace. You may feel challenged at times, but you won't continually be frustrated.

Know Thyself

One of the great secrets of success is to find out your abilities and limitations and go from there. In other words, *know thyself!* God created those abilities within you, and He wants to use them to His glory. On the other hand, unless you have specifically heard from God to do otherwise, don't go beyond your limitations. As I said, you will be frustrated if you do.

I understand my personal limitations, and that's why I surround myself with staff members who have what I don't have. I am a visionary, a motivator, and a promoter. I know that. But I need people around me who can take the vision God gives me and put together a plan or a program to help that vision come to pass. They are the "engineers," if you will, who are gifted at taking my vision and putting together a plan to carry out the vision.

When you find out who you really are, and you begin to operate in those channels, things will go well for you. That's hard for some people to accept because they don't want to admit that there are some areas they are simply not gifted in. Maybe they get down on themselves or feel inferior if they can't do something as well as somebody else can. But they need to realize that God is their Creator; He doesn't make any mistakes—and He doesn't make inferior creations!

Jesus Himself said, "I pray not that thou [God the Father] shouldest take them out of the world, but that thou shouldest keep them from the evil. THEY ARE NOT OF THE WORLD, even as I am not of the world" (John 17:15,16 *KJV*).

We are *in* the world, but we are not *of* the world!

As I said, human beings, though limited in themselves, have the unique ability as believers to live in two realms at the same time. When we become born again, we gain citizenship in Heaven. We participate in a divine exchange, if you will, in which limited man meets *un*limited God in a divine relationship, and our impossibilities can become God's *possibilities* in the earth!

Chapter 7

WHAT IT MEANS TO BE 'WITH GOD'

In the last chapter, we looked at the first part of Luke 18:27: *"The things which are impossible with men . . ." (KJV)*. Now let's look at the last part of that verse.

LUKE 18:27 (KJV)

27 The things which are impossible with men are possible **WITH GOD.**

We all like to hear about man's possibilities with God. But exactly what does the phrase "with God" mean? We know that to believers, "with God" can certainly mean being born again. In the New Birth, He is not only *with* us but *in* us. However, there's more to receiving and walking in God's blessings and His greater glory. Certainly, in the New Birth, we become qualified as partakers of God's divine nature and as heirs of God and joint-heirs with Jesus. But how do we actually *partake* of the blessings and glory of God? How do we receive and experience them for ourselves?

A Lifestyle, Not an Event

So many people accept Jesus Christ as Savior, and then that's *that*. They don't receive Him as *Lord* of their lives. They don't go any deeper in their walk with Him. They go back to living their lives the best they know how and waiting for the Sweet By-and-By when they'll walk those heavenly streets of gold. But the "with God" that makes man's impossibilities possible also means that we're following Him. In other words, our being "with God" is a lifestyle, not just an event.

Let's look further at Luke 18:27 and the verses that follow.

LUKE 18:27–30

27 Jesus replied, "What is impossible with men is possible with God."

28 Peter said to him, "We have left all we had to follow you!"

29 "I tell you the truth," Jesus said to them, "no one who has left home or wife or brothers or parents or children for the sake of the kingdom of God

30 will fail to receive many times as much in this age and, in the age to come, eternal life."

Talking about himself and the other disciples, Peter said to Jesus, "We have left everything to follow You."

Did you know that to follow God sometimes means giving up some things or making a sacrifice? It may mean leaving a group of friends you've been associating with who don't want to wholeheartedly follow God. It may mean moving to a certain place in obedience to Him and giving up the comfort of familiar surroundings. It could mean any number of things. But if you will follow God with your whole heart, He will give you more than you ever had before.

When Peter said to Jesus, "We've left everything to follow You," notice Jesus' reply: ". . . No one who has done these things will fail to receive many times as much in this age and then, in the age to come, eternal life" (vv. 29,30).

You never give up anything for God that He won't prosper and bless you many times more as a result. But sometimes, people want to see the *blessing* before they do the *giving up*. That's where faith comes in. You have to believe Luke 18:27–30: that the God who does the impossible will increase you in every area of your life as you follow after Him. So don't just sit around and try to figure out with your head, your natural human intellect, whether or not God will bless you. Just follow Him with all your heart. Obey Him in everything you do, and the blessings will come.

What It Means to Follow God

We know that if we're "with God," we're following Him. But let's break that down further. What does it mean to follow God? For one, it means that if we're "with God," we have priorities—not *our* priorities, but *His*.

If you were to take a course in time management, one of the first things you'd learn is that you need to prioritize your activities, tasks, and goals to get a clearer picture of the things that are most important in your life. Then you could devote more of your time to those things.

Following` God Means
Putting First Things First

When God's priorities become your priorities, you will put Him and His Word first in your life. And it's not an option; it's a necessity. You won't put friends first. You won't put listening to tapes, reading teaching materials, or attending special meetings first. You will put *Him* first! Those other things can help you, but they can't take the place of the unadulterated Word of God and of your fellowship with Him.

You can always tell when a person is putting God and His Word first in his or her life. It's not the absence of tests or trials that determines whether a person is putting God first. *It's what that person does in the midst of a test or trial that shows where his or her priorities lie.* When you're putting God first, you won't wring your hands and worry, saying, "Oh, God, what am I going to do?" No, you will have already armed yourself with the Word of God, and you will begin to speak it out. What you have placed in your heart will eventually come out of your mouth.

Have you ever noticed that when a sponge becomes saturated with water or some other liquid, it's not always easy to recognize it until you squeeze the sponge? Then whatever is in that sponge comes pouring out. In much the same way, when the pressures of life come against you, whatever your heart is full of will come pouring out of your mouth.

Another aspect of putting first things first is not only putting God and His *Word* first, but putting His *will* first. If we are going to follow God, we are going to have to put His desires above our desires and choose His will for our lives over our own.

The choice to put God's will for our lives first is a decision that we will have to reaffirm throughout our lives. The decision to do the will of God takes continual dedication and consecration; it's not just something we say to the Lord one time, and that's it.

If you haven't already done so, I challenge you to put God's desires for your life first, above your own. He made you and has created you for a very special purpose. You can trust Him to cause that purpose to be fulfilled in your life. And it will be better than anything you could have planned on your own.

Following God Means Being Led by the Spirit of God

We've seen that if we're really "with God"—if we're really following Him—*number one*, we're putting first things first; we're putting God, His Word, and His will first. And *number two*, we're learning to be led by the Spirit of God.

You can train yourself to be sensitive to the Greater One within you, the Holy Ghost, and to follow His leading, even if your mind wants to do something else. For example, have you ever been in a situation in which your heart, or your spirit, was saying one thing, but your mind was saying something else? Sometimes your mind can scream at you, especially when the pressure is on. But when you get quiet and begin to listen to what the Holy Spirit is saying to your spirit, you will know what to do. Your mind will argue, *Yes, but I can't figure that out. I just don't see how that can work out.*

But, friend, you don't always have to have everything figured out! Follow the Spirit of God, and He will always lead you in line with the Word to victory and success.

Following God Means Committing Yourself Wholeheartedly to Him

In review, how do we know we're really following God and positioning ourselves to receive His blessings and walk in His greater glory? *Number one*, we're putting God, His Word, and His will first. And *number two*, we're learning to be led by the Spirit of God.

Now, *number three*, following God means that we are *committed* to following Him as a lifestyle. We are *committed* to putting Him, His Word, and His will first on a continual basis. And we are *committed* to following the leading of the Holy Spirit.

We need to have the attitude that we are going to wholeheartedly commit ourselves—"live, die, sink, or swim"—to following the One who knows more about us than we know about ourselves and who cares more about whether we prosper and succeed than we do! He has our best interests at heart; we can trust Him with our life!

The Rewards of Following God

We've learned what it means to be "with God" and to follow Him. We know that if we are "with God," we are *putting God, His Word, and His will* first; we are *learning to be led by the Spirit of God*; and we are *committed to doing these things,* despite the sacrifices we think we may have to make to do them.

Whatever you think you may be sacrificing to follow God is nothing compared to the rewards of following Him. Whatever you leave behind in order to obey Him is nothing compared to what you will receive from Him, both in this life and the next (1 Tim. 4:8).

Someone might argue, "Well, you sound so certain, but I'm just not sure." People like that often find themselves feeling dissatisfied and unfulfilled. They're *questioning* rather than *believing.* They haven't reached the point in their walk where they can say with full assurance of faith, "God said it. I believe it. That settles it!"

When the pressures and tests and trials of life come and try to steal from us and make us doubt, we have to let the infallible truth of God's Word be our rock and the foundation on which we stand. We have to maintain our commitment to following God, His Word, and His will for our lives no matter what. And we have to steadfastly follow the leading of His Spirit.

No Way Out

Many Christians will start out believing God when they're in a test or trial. They study God's Word just a little bit. But when the circumstances don't improve, they give up. They're not *committed* to God and His Word. But to receive the full measure of God's blessing—to partake of and participate in His greater glory—we're going to have to do our homework spiritually. We're going to have to dig deep into the Word and obey what we find that He has told us to do. Then having done all to stand, we must stand *and then stand some more* (Eph. 6:13)! We must stand our ground, no matter how badly we may be hurting on the inside, knowing that God will not let us down.

Your heart may be broken and your mind may be shouting at the top of its voice, *You're not going to make it! There is no way out of this!* You may have to bite your lip to keep from giving in to hysteria and desperation. You may have to just close your eyes and cling in faith to the Master, because all you can see is blackness, bleakness, and hopelessness with no way out. But if you will hold to the truth that the answer to your problem is possible with God, you will make it through! You will come out of that test or trial and experience the sunshine of God's blessing.

Jesus' disciples experienced a "no way out" situation of their own. In the midst of their stormy trial, it looked as if they were doomed and that there was no way out of their situation.

Mark chapter 4, records that Jesus climbed onboard a ship with His disciples and told them, ". . . Let us go over to the other side" (v. 35). Then Jesus went to the back of the ship, laid down, and went to sleep.

You'll remember that a great storm arose. The wind and waves were so fierce that the ship began to be tossed about, and the disciples became afraid for their lives. They awoke the Master, screaming out, "Don't You care that we're going to die!" (v. 38).

Jesus got up, rebuked the wind, and said to His disciples, ". . . how is it that ye have no faith?" (Mark 4:40 KJV).

We know that faith begins where the will of God is known. Well, Jesus had just said, "Let us go over to the other side." Those were the words of the Master, the Living Word! The will of God had been revealed in Jesus' words, "Let us go over to the other side." When Jesus said those words, He meant exactly that! He meant, "Let us go over to the other side," not, "Let us go a distance and die on our way to the other side."

Jesus fully expected to go to the other side. He believed the words that He had spoken, and He fully expected those words to come to pass. The disciples should have believed them too. But they didn't. Instead, they were filled with fear, and Jesus had to rebuke them, saying, in effect, "Why don't you have any faith?"

Did you know that as you journey on your ship across life's ocean, you are going to be beset with storms and tests that will arise to challenge what God has spoken to you from His Word? What are you going to do? Are you going to throw up your hands and cry, "Lord, don't You care about what I'm going through!"? Or are you going to recognize the fact that He has made a way of escape out of that trial? You can stand in the face of the winds and waves of adversity and declare, "When it's impossible with me, it's still possible with God!"

Trusting in Self Will Keep You Under— Trusting in God Will Put You Over!

I never said it would be easy to boldly declare your faith when the howling winds of adversity are blowing, threatening to destroy you. But Jesus has already said, in effect, "Put your hand in Mine. The things that are impossible with you are possible with Me."

Yet how many times do we panic and give way to fear and doubt, leaning to our own understanding instead of trusting in Him (Prov. 3:5)?

In the midst of a test or trial, leaning to your own understanding and trusting in yourself will not deliver you. In fact, your own understanding will put you in fear, doubt, and condemnation. Your own understanding will give you a defeatist attitude. Your own understanding will keep you under the problem! But trusting in God and His Word will put you on top!

Focusing on the Father

Let's look at another verse in the Gospels that goes right along with our text, Luke 18:27.

MARK 10:27
27 Jesus looked at them and said, "With man this is impossible, but not WITH GOD; all things are possible WITH GOD."

With God. Notice Jesus didn't say, "All things are possible with man," or "All things are possible if you stay positive and believe you can get it done somehow," or "All things are possible in your own strength." No, Jesus' focus was on the Father; He talked the "natural" right out of that verse!

The Apostle Paul wrote, "I can do everything through him [Christ] who gives me strength" (Phil. 4:13). We can't do "everything" in our own strength, but whatever our God-given task, we can do it through Christ, who gives us the strength we need. We are strong in the Lord and in the power of His might (Eph. 6:10).

As I said, God never intended that we try to make it on our own. Instead, He wants to turn our *impossibilities* into His *possibilities* as we follow Him and put ourselves in position to receive His blessings and His glory. We need to learn to "let go and let God" and allow His power to take us over to the other side of our sea of problems and tests.

The following is a prophetic utterance I received from the Lord as I ministered in a church setting along these same lines. It applies to all of us today.

> Forget the past.
>
> The problem with you and the reason you're not succeeding is
>
> You're turning around and listening to the voices of the past.
>
> Forget the voices of the past and grab hold of what I've spoken to you through My servant, and never look back again.
>
> But 'with God,' begin to march forward.

'With God,' begin to take the land.

'With God,' begin to do what you know you can do!

'With God,' become the success that I want you to become,

Both minister and layman.

I say to you, '*I Am* God, and *with Me*, you cannot fail!'

As you take hold of the truth that your impossibilities can become possibilities *with Him*, give voice to that truth by confessing it out loud and by rejoicing in Him. The Spirit of God will begin to work in your life to cause you to walk in a greater and greater measure of God's glory and blessing. Your praise will give way to God's power, and as "limited" meets "*un*limited," things will begin to change for the better.

And as you trust in the Lord with all your heart and lean not to your own understanding, you'll begin to get a new mindset, a new way of thinking. Then when your mind screams at you, *Impossible*, out of your spirit, a different cry will arise: *Possible with God!* Obstacles will be moved and you'll receive the breakthroughs you need so that the plan of God can go forth in your life, and you can experience greater manifestations of His glory.

Chapter 8

ASPECTS OF
THE PRESENCE OF GOD

When it comes to understanding the Presence of the Lord, too many people are in a ditch on one side of the road or the other (as is the case with many Bible subjects), while the truth is right down the middle!

Take, for example, those believers who are so hyper-spiritual that they become difficult to relate to in the natural. They can't even carry on a normal conversation about the weather, for example, without saying something flaky or weird. To them, everything that happens has some kind of spiritual meaning or connotation to it, and they get off-base doctrinally; they get off in the ditch on one side of the road concerning spirituality.

These people are what some call being "so heavenly minded that they're no earthly good." And it's true. They're not doing much for the Kingdom of God, because they always have their head in the clouds, so to speak. They can't relate to most people, and most people can't relate to them. They don't enjoy life at all, and others usually do not enjoy being around them.

Then in the ditch on the other side of that road, there are those who are so earthly minded and who are caught up so much in natural things that they're not attuned to spiritual things at all. They have no power of God working in their lives. They know all the latest news, trends, and Hollywood gossip, but they can't point someone else to God, because they are shallow spiritually and have very little knowledge of God or the Bible.

Can you see now why I said the truth is somewhere in the middle?

Concerning the Presence of God, some people have the idea that we can't access the Presence of God. Their concept of God's Presence is this: "Man is down here, and God is up there, and there is a great distance between the two. We just have to get along down here as best we can."

Other people fall into the category I spoke about previously— the hyper-spiritual people who think God's Presence and spiritual gifts should be in manifestation all the time. For example, they are either always looking for a special word from the Lord, such as a prophecy, or they're always giving out "words from the Lord." Many times, they're just speaking out of their own souls, not by the Spirit of God. Bless their hearts, they're trying to be spiritual, but they're trying to do it by leaning to their own understanding! They're being naturally "spiritual" instead of being *supernaturally spiritual*. There's a big difference.

There is a right way and a wrong way to relate to the Presence of God. In this chapter, we are going to explore from the Word of God the right way to relate to His Presence.

Three Aspects of the Presence of God

Some people become confused when you talk about getting in the Presence of God, and they will ask, "Well, I'm a Christian; isn't the Presence of God already *in* and *with* me? Why do I need to *'get in His Presence'*?"

In other words, they're asking, "How do you get in the presence of God when His Presence is already in and with you?"

Yes, the Presence of God is *in* and *with* us as believers. But that doesn't mean that we can't also experience manifestations of the Presence of God *upon* us!

You know, in the area of prayer, people have believed that all praying is the same. But the Bible teaches that there are several kinds of praying and that there are different rules governing each kind. As my father said many times, when it comes to prayer, people just sort of lump all types of prayer together in one sack, shake them up, and pour them all out together. And that's why the prayers of many aren't working—they are using the wrong rules and laws.

And Dad was right. You can't play football with baseball rules, and you can't pray the prayer of faith, for example, using the scriptural rules or guidelines for praying the prayer of consecration! When praying the prayer of faith, you believe you receive, and you thank God that you have *right now*—by faith—whatever you asked Him for (*see* Mark 11:24). Then you continue to thank Him for the answer.

But when praying the prayer of consecration, you are praying, "Not my will, Lord, but Yours be done" (*see* Luke 22:42). You are committing your way to Him and your will to His will. It is a different kind of praying altogether. There is also the prayer of agreement, the prayer of commitment (the prayer of casting your care on the Lord), and so forth.

That's one of the reasons why some people have so many problems getting their prayers answered. They don't understand that there are different rules that go with different kinds of prayer. I think the same is true concerning the Presence of God. We haven't understood the subject properly.

There are three aspects of the Presence of God that I want to look at in this chapter: (1) God is *omnipresent*, (2) God's Presence can be *indwelling*, and (3) God's Presence can be *manifested*.

Number One: God Is *Omnipresent*

Let's look at the first aspect of the Presence of God: God is *omnipresent*. That simply means that He is present everywhere at all times.

PSALM 139:7,8

7 **Where can I go from your Spirit? Where can I flee from your presence?**

8 If I go up to the heavens, you are there; if I make my bed in the depths, you are there.

The Psalmist was saying, in effect, "The Presence of God is everywhere." In that sense, we could say that *everyone* is in the Presence of God. We could conclude then that because God is present in the earth, God's Presence is also down at such-and-such a bar, for example.

We could correctly come to that conclusion, but that doesn't mean people at the bar are receiving anything from God's Presence, because you'd have to tap into that Presence to receive from Him. But if someone at that bar called on the Name of the Lord, he or she could receive from Him, because God is present everywhere, at all times.

We as Christians should be especially conscious and aware of God's omnipresence. He is in and with us as believers— and He is also ever-present everywhere! He is present in our homes, on our jobs, as we're driving our cars, as we're shopping, and as we're enjoying the outdoors or doing whatever it is we like to do for recreation. But how many of us are tapping into that power that is available to us "24–7"? Could it be because His omnipresence is not a living reality to us?

You see, if God were not present everywhere at all times— or *omnipresent*—you couldn't witness to someone out on the street and get him or her born again. You'd have to bring that person to a special place where the Presence of God was, because the Holy Spirit, or God's Presence, must be present in the New Birth. It is He who baptizes that convert into Christ, into the Body of Christ, and makes his or her spirit brand-new.

We know that you could witness to someone anywhere on the earth, and if that person believes the Word that is given to him or her and calls upon the Name of the Lord, that person will be saved (Rom. 10:13)!

God is present everywhere. But if we're going to experience the glory and Presence of God, we're going to have to tap into His Presence. And He has given us His Word so that we wouldn't be in the dark concerning how to relate to His omnipresence.

Number Two:
God's Presence Can Be *Indwelling*

So, first, we have seen that God is *omnipresent*, or present everywhere at all times. Second, God's Presence can be *indwelling*. God's Presence indwells the believing ones, those who have accepted Jesus Christ as their Savior and Lord.

JOHN 14:16,17

16 "And I will ask the Father, and he will give you another Counselor to be with you forever—

17 the Spirit of truth. The world cannot accept him, because it neither sees him nor knows him. But you know him, for he lives WITH you and will be IN you."

These verses in John 14 bear out what we have already discussed in chapter 2: every believer is a temple of the indwelling Presence of God.

The Apostle Paul said something similar in First Corinthians 6:19: "Do you not know that your body is a temple of the Holy Spirit, who is *in* you, whom you have received from God? You are not your own." Clearly, God's Presence indwells us—lives in us—as believers.

Number Three:
God's Presence Can Be *Manifested*

Concerning the Presence of God, we learned first that God is omnipotent, and, second, that His Presence indwells believers in Jesus Christ. Now, third, we will see that the Presence of God can be *manifested*. God manifests His Presence in the earth in and through people to bless people and to accomplish certain things in their lives.

For example, another wave of revival began in the 1990s as many in the Church experienced manifestations of God's Presence with displays of joy. God manifested Himself to bless people. When people yielded to the manifestation of the Spirit, they would laugh, dance, jump, or run under the influence and inspiration of the Holy Spirit.

Now, the Holy Spirit can manifest Himself in any way He chooses at any time. For example, I'm sure there were people who received healing by a manifestation of the Spirit before and after the Healing Revival of the '40s and '50s. But *during* that revival, those things happened more often. And it seemed it was easier for people to get healed by their own faith.

Don't misunderstand me. You can be healed by your faith at any time, because healing was purchased for you in redemption. Healing is yours for the taking; you can receive healing right now by faith in God's holy, unchanging Word. But back in the days of that Healing Revival, my father would be in meetings in which the glory of God would manifest, and every sick person in the building would be supernaturally healed. Every unsaved person would spontaneously run to the altar and give his or her life to God. And everyone present who hadn't received the baptism in the Holy Spirit with the evidence of speaking in other tongues would instantly begin speaking in tongues and giving glory to God!

God was manifesting Himself during that time for a purpose. It didn't mean people could only receive healing, salvation, or the baptism in the Holy Spirit when the glory of God was in manifestation. Certainly not! It just meant that when there was a powerful manifestation of God's Presence, it seemed as if things just happened; it was easier to receive under that strong anointing.

I've been in meetings with Dad when the glory of God manifested, and Dad would begin preaching rapid-fire for 40 minutes or longer under a powerful anointing of the Spirit. Scripture after scripture seemed to roll out of his mouth, and afterward, he'd have to get the tape to hear what he said!

Those were supernatural manifestations of God's Presence. The people would sit riveted under the anointing of the Spirit, and they'd be blessed, healed, and set free as the glory of God came down upon them.

In the manifest Presence of God, heart's desires are met, problems are solved, and lives are changed!

In your personal prayer life, have you ever begun sensing something the Lord was trying to get over to you, but at that moment, it wasn't quite clear? When the glory of God is manifested, direction may suddenly become vivid. In His manifest Presence is where you can receive answers to questions that have nagged you for some time. Those answers become evident in the light of the glory of God.

We Need to Embrace, Not Shun, God's Manifest Presence

Some pastors—even some so-called Charismatic pastors—have a problem with Christians acting "wild" in church. They don't like all the shouting and dancing and running. But if they knew why some of those people acted that way, they would be shouting for joy, too! Some have had the sentence of death pronounced upon them. Doctors told them there was no hope for their condition. But they were healed by the power of God!

Others were addicted to drugs and alcohol, but were delivered by the power of God. Others were delivered from all kinds of bondage and oppression.

Once you've come out on the other side of the darkness that has held you bound, you can't *help* but praise and thank God for your many blessings! Even if you've never suffered the cruel oppression of the enemy, after you've lived for

God awhile, you just want to thank and praise Him for His goodness and faithfulness! You want to rejoice because of His great love! You want to shout because His mercies are new every morning! You want to worship Him because He rewards those who diligently seek Him!

The Ministry of Jesus Was 'Seeker Friendly'!

We are living in a day when the "seeker friendly" church is gaining popularity. Some of these churches no longer believe in calling sin *sin*. They downplay sin and wrongdoing, and they don't say much about Heaven or hell. Songs about the Blood have become obsolete, and all of this is done with the intent of not making anyone "uncomfortable" or uneasy.

Jesus said that He came to seek and save those who were lost (Luke 19:10). But if we make no spiritual plea to the lost to become saved, there is little reason for the power of God to be in manifestation in our churches.

In our preaching and teaching, we have to get back to urging people everywhere that there is a Heaven to gain and a hell to shun. If we don't, and if we continue to make it "comfortable" for the world inside our church walls, we may lose the move of God in this generation.

Certainly, we are to welcome the lost into our churches with open arms. We want to draw them, but we want them to be drawn by the power and Spirit of God, for He is their only hope of eternal salvation. We don't need programs that water down the Word of God to draw people. Jesus said, "If *I* be lifted up, *I* will draw all men unto Me" (John 12:32).

A Charge to Pastors

I think many pastors have allowed church programs to distract them from a true move of the Spirit of God. Don't misunderstand me. I'm not against all church programs. Some of these programs help people, and they are a blessing. But sometimes, they can hinder us if we're not careful. If we allow programs to take the place of the true move of the Spirit, it will be a sad day indeed when we finally look around to see nothing but sweat and toil—nothing but the work of man's hands—instead of what God Almighty is doing in the earth!

In the day in which we are living, there are church buildings filled every week with people who are hearing nice sermons, but what they hear doesn't affect their lives or impact the world. There's no power in many churches today, even Charismatic churches.

Some are seeking prosperity for themselves and are contributing little or nothing to missions or other outreaches that are bringing the lost into the Kingdom, into the saving knowledge of Jesus Christ. And it seems that some pastors are more concerned about not offending people and trying to get their church attendance up than about building the Kingdom of God *His* way. As I said, they no longer mention the "blood," referring to the shed blood of Jesus Christ, for fear of making someone uncomfortable.

I heard one pastor say, "Well, when the most prominent businessman in town is at my church, I just can't afford to have any speaking in tongues in the service. He may never come back."

That businessman probably knew before he ever set foot in the place that the people in that church spoke in tongues. In fact, that may have been why he went there to begin with! Like so many others in the world today, he's looking for an answer. But if all he's given is the same "six and seven" that he's used to, he's not going to get any answers. His spiritual hunger will not be satisfied, and he won't go back to that church, anyway.

The enemy knows his time is short, and in these last days, he is going to try to pull everyone away from God that he can. The Bible says even some of the "elect," those who've been born again by the blood of the Lamb, will be pulled away (Matt. 24:24; Mark 13:22). I see this happening in some so-called Charismatic churches that have experienced God's glory in the past, but have grown indifferent to the move of the Spirit.

Some ministers object: "Well, what if in yielding to the Holy Spirit, I make a mistake?"

God would rather have your mistakes than your indifference!

When believers resist opportunity after opportunity to go with God and with what He's doing in the earth, I believe they can be pulled away more easily. They can become numb to spiritual things, unable to discern those things as they should.

I'm not saying any of this to be critical, but to help. And I'm not talking about something I've heard about but haven't witnessed for myself. I have actually ministered in services in which the power of God was in strong manifestation to bless, heal, and set people free. Yet because the pastor had instructed me that demonstrations of the power of God were reserved for another type of service to be held at another time, I had to turn the service back over to him.

Someone asked, "Well, if you sensed a moving of the Spirit in the service, why didn't you just go ahead and yield to it, regardless of what the pastor told you to do?"

Because when I am invited as a guest minister in someone else's church, I am under the auspices of that pastor. The pastor, not a visiting minister, has authority in his or her church. You can't go against that without getting into an area of disobedience with God, because God has set the pastor to be the head of a local church body.

Once, I ministered in someone else's church on a Sunday morning, and the pastor had said to me that he didn't want any manifestations of the Spirit in the morning service. Well, from the moment I began preaching, I sensed a strong anointing of the Spirit of God, and I knew that God wanted to do some things in that service. But when I finished my message, I had to turn the service back over to the pastor, who proceeded to give a casual invitation to anyone who wanted to know more about Jesus or who wanted to change his way of life.

I was also scheduled to preach that evening at what was going to be one of those services for which the power of God had been "reserved." That evening, I preached with all the gusto and enthusiasm I could muster—I mean, I pulled out all the stops—and the service seemed as dead and dry as it could be in terms of the moving of the Spirit! I preached harder than I'd ever preached before, and there simply wasn't the moving of the Spirit that I had sensed in the morning service.

"Why was that?" someone asked.

Because you can't tell the Spirit of God when He can move and cannot move!

Born in the Fire

I once heard a respected minister say "Pentecostalism was born in the fire, but if we're not careful, it will die in the smoke."

Have you ever seen what happens after a fire goes out? Usually, a bunch of smoke comes up. But did you ever notice that if you begin to fan the smoke and embers, you can often bring that fire back to life?

I believe that in this day, the wind of the Spirit is blowing on individual members of the Church and on the Church as a whole to fan the embers of His moving among us into brightly burning flames. May we each yield to Him and allow the fires of His manifest Presence to burn strongly in our midst.

Chapter 9

OBEDIENCE
AND THE GLORY

My father lived a life of faith, consecration, and obedience before the Lord. Not only was he 100 percent dedicated to doing the Lord's will, he was diligent—diligent to study, diligent to pray and to seek God's face, and diligent to obey the Word and the direction he received from the Lord.

And my father saw great results in his ministry. He experienced marvelous moves of the Spirit of God. Dad saw the glory cloud many times, and had many spectacular experiences with the Spirit of God.[1] And as I said previously, we of this generation need to take the torch that he and others like him were so faithful to carry and with it and through our own obedience, set the world on fire with the power and glory of God!

In this chapter and in following chapters, I am going to share with you nine keys for entering into and experiencing a greater measure of the glory of God. We've already read about some of the manifestations of God's glory in modern history and learned a little about how God was able to move in such a glorious way in those instances. And we've also seen in the Bible many of the numerous instances in which God displayed His glory.

Let's take a closer look at some of those Bible instances and discover the keys that caused God's glory to be manifested.

LEVITICUS 9:5,6,23

5 **They took the things Moses commanded to the front of the Tent of Meeting, and the entire assembly came near and stood before the Lord.**

6 **Then Moses said, "THIS IS WHAT THE LORD HAS COMMANDED YOU TO DO, SO THAT THE GLORY OF THE LORD MAY APPEAR TO YOU."**

23 **Moses and Aaron then went into the Tent of Meeting. When they came out, they blessed the people; and the glory of the Lord appeared to all the people.**

Notice in verse 23 it says, "Moses and Aaron went into the Tent of Meeting. . . ." You see, in the Old Testament, the people couldn't go into the place where the Presence of God dwelt. Only the prophet, priest, and king were allowed to go before God. They often entered God's Presence *on behalf of* the people, but the population at large could not enter what they called the Holy Place.

Because of Jesus, We Have Access to the Glory of God

Think about that! Although the prophet, priest, and king could enter the Holy Place, they could do so only after going through a special cleansing process. And even when they did experience manifestations of the power and Presence of God—God's glory—they only experienced Him outwardly, on a lower dimension than we as believers are capable of experiencing Him today.

And what gives us the right to experience the Presence of God as we do? We don't have to undergo any special ceremony to enter His Presence, because the blood of Jesus Christ has made us clean, holy, and righteous. It is through Him that we have access to the glory of God. We should be ever mindful and thankful of that great fact!

Not only did the prophet, priest, and king have to be ceremonially cleansed before entering the Holy Place, but even then, they didn't have direct access to the glory of God. Only the High Priest could go into that inner place, the Holy of Holies, where the Ark of God resided. The High Priest went in once a year on behalf of all the people. And he had to follow precisely the instructions God had given, or he would die.

Jewish tradition bears out the fact that the High Priest had golden bells attached to the hem of his garment. If the bells stopped tinkling while he was in the Holy Place, it was an indication that he had died because he failed to follow God's instructions for entering His Presence. Those who were outside the Holy of Holies would then literally drag the High Priest out with a rope that was tied around his ankle.

God is a holy God, and you couldn't enter His Presence in an unholy manner. Strict obedience to God's regulations was the rule, and if anyone did not obey those regulations set up under the Law, he brought himself under certain judgment.

Thank God, Jesus has made a new and living way (Heb. 10:20) for us to approach that same holy God and have access to His Presence and glory. Let's begin looking at keys to experiencing that glory for ourselves and to entering into greater and greater measures of God's glory.

Key Number One: *Obey God*

Key number one to experiencing God's greater glory is *obedience*. We already read in Leviticus 9:6, that Moses said, ". . . 'This is what the Lord has commanded you to do, so that the glory of the Lord may appear to you.'" If you read verses 8 through 22, you'll find that Aaron the priest obeyed and offered the sin offering for the people "in the prescribed way" (v. 16). And we know it must have been acceptable to God, because verse 23 says, "Moses and Aaron then went into the Tent of Meeting. When they came out, they blessed the people; *and the glory of the Lord appeared to all the people.*"

The glory of the Lord appeared! You see, if we're going to experience God's greater glory, we're going to have to obey Him. We have to obey what He says to do in His Word, because God's Word is God speaking to us. We also have to obey Him specifically when He speaks to us. When we do these things, the glory of the Lord will appear, and God will manifest Himself in a greater measure than we've experienced before.

What happens many times is that we'll hear God speaking something to our heart that He wants us to do, and we'll only *partially* obey it because we're too busy with our own plan, or what God is saying doesn't fit in with our plans. But obedience without compromise is the key to experiencing the greater glory.

God may speak to you about some things you need to change in your personal life. He may speak to a pastor about changing the format of his church services. He may speak to someone else about his prayer time, because he's not doing everything God told him to do concerning prayer.

Let's look at a New Testament scripture about obedience.

JOHN 14:21

21 **"Whoever has my commands and obeys them, he is the one who loves me. He who loves me will be loved by my Father, and I too will love him AND SHOW MYSELF TO HIM."**

Yes, we have to want the glory. We have to hunger and seek God for it. But we also have to *obey* Him. The key to the greater glory is obedience to God in everything, *including changing whatever needs to be changed*, so that we can experience the full measure of God's blessing and power.

Don't Break the Pattern and Miss the Blessing!

Obedience to God puts us in position for God to bless us and display His glory in our lives. When we obey Him, we put ourselves in God's "pattern" so He can bless us.

To give you a natural illustration, if I were playing football, and the quarterback told me to run a certain pattern, then I would have to run that pattern as practiced so I would be in the right position on the field. If I broke that pattern and went somewhere on the field that I wasn't supposed to go, I could cost my team the opportunity to score.

Have you ever heard a sports announcer say, "The receiver broke the pattern, and the pass was no good"? That receiver wasn't where he was supposed to be on the field.

There are believers who have received specific instructions from God concerning something they are supposed to do. But then they get distracted and forget what He said. Pretty soon, they don't hear anything from God when they pray. Things aren't working out for them the way they think they should, and they wonder why God isn't blessing them.

They're not receiving God's blessings because they're out of position. They've broken the pattern, so to speak.

Then there are other believers who haven't necessarily received any specific instructions from God, yet they have *general* instructions from God's Word that they're not obeying. Remember, God's Word is God speaking to us. And His Word says that we are to forgive others and walk in love. If we're not doing that, we've broken the pattern; we're out of position to receive God's best.

The Word also tells us not to forsake the assembling of ourselves together (Heb. 10:25). Yet so many Christians are sitting at home on Sunday mornings instead of attending their local church. They might even be at home watching a good Christian teaching program, but they're still not obeying God's instructions in His Word. They've broken the pattern, and they've made it difficult for God to bless them and show Himself strong in their lives as He desires.

The Bible also instructs us to feed the hungry, to give to the poor, and to do good to one another. Now, certainly, we are to be concerned about feeding the hungry who are unsaved, because it's difficult for someone to receive the Gospel when he doesn't have enough food to eat and he's starving physically. But I'm also talking about feeding the hungry who are inside the church walls. There are believers all around us who are in need. We as believers need to give as we are able and meet the needs of others, including other believers.

In a previous chapter, I alluded to the fact that obedience is an act of faith and of cooperation with God and His Word. In other words, if you really believe God is who He says He is, you will do what He says to do.

A passage in James chapter 2 also bears this out.

JAMES 2:14–17

14 **What good is it, my brothers, if a man claims to have faith but has no deeds? Can such faith save him?**

15 **Suppose a brother or sister is without clothes and daily food.**

16 **If one of you says to him, "Go, I wish you well; keep warm and well fed," but does nothing about his physical needs, what good is it?**

17 **In the same way, faith by itself, if it is not accompanied by action, is dead.**

If we look the other way when others are in need, we can't claim to be walking in faith and in obedience to God. According to these verses, the measure of a person's faith in God is his deeds, or his obedience to God. And, remember, God and His Word are One. So if you're going to be obedient to God, you have to obey His Word. And His Word is clear here that if we have the wherewithal to help someone in need, we are supposed to help them.

Many people will help someone else only if it doesn't inconvenience them too much or involve too much sacrifice. I remember I was preaching in a meeting once, and the Lord led me to give $100 to a young man who was just starting out in full-time ministry. I happened to have $100 in my billfold. It was my "hide" money. I call it that, because I always try to keep some cash hidden away for something I might need or want. (My wife knows about my "hide" money, but some husbands won't admit that they keep some "hide" money somewhere, even if it's just a small amount, that they can use just for themselves!) At the time, that $100 was all I had, and I wasn't at the place financially where I could just replace it instantly.

This young man had been ministered to in a prayer line. He had fallen under the power of God and was lying on the floor as God was ministering to Him by the anointing. I bent down quietly and put that money in his shirt pocket. That's the way the Lord led me to do it.

When I traveled, I usually bought gifts to take home to my son and daughter. But I had just given away all the money I had. Yet to me, it was more important to obey the leading of the Lord than to be selfish with my money. (Actually, since it was God who gave it to me to begin with, it really wasn't mine to do with just as I pleased, anyway).

I'm not telling you this to try to bring any glory to myself. I'm simply using myself as an example to make a point, because I know myself better than someone else I might use as an example!

After I gave that $100 to the young minister in obedience to the Lord, someone blessed me with some extra money to buy gifts for my children. But I didn't give that money in order to get money. I did it just because the Lord told me to do it, and He blessed me as a result.

As I've said many times, the blessings of God don't come to us just because we want them. We have to position ourselves to receive from God, and that includes receiving the greater glory. And we position ourselves to receive through our obedience.

God Has a Plan!

Some people will obey God to an extent. They will attend church and maybe even pay tithes. But then they want God to leave them alone concerning His specific plan for their lives. They are comfortable in their job or career, and they don't want to hear that they may not be doing in life exactly what God has planned for them to do.

In a previous chapter, I said that following God meant putting His desires and His will above our own, and doing that may mean giving up some things. To obey God fully, you may need to give up *your* idea about what you want to do in life, such as following a career path that you have chosen.

In talking to young people, I always encourage them to pray and get God's plan *before* they begin planning their life. Then they can find out what God would have them do and begin following that path without having to change paths down the road somewhere.

To be wholly submitted to God and wholly obedient to Him takes faith. You have to be more committed to God, Whom you can't see, than to the things that you can see. Our walk with Him is a journey of faith. But we will do well if we are obedient to Him!

The devil will always try to distract you from following God's plan for your life. If he can't get you to willfully rebel against God, he will try to trip you up with sin so that your spirit is held captive to the will of your flesh.

If he can't lead you off into sin, he will try to distract you with other things, even things that aren't necessarily bad or wrong. For example, it may be a tempting job offer, but you know in your heart that if you accept it, it will take you further from the will of God for your life instead of bringing you closer. It could be a wrong relationship that the enemy uses to try and distract you. Or it could simply be a hobby that begins taking up so much of your time that you're not spending enough time in God's Word, fellowshipping with him.

Before I answered the call to the ministry, I was planning to be a meteorologist. I also wanted to race cars. In fact, I once owned a race car, but my wife wouldn't let me drive it much! I raced it just as a hobby for two years and then I finally sold it.

A couple of years before I bought that car, a friend and I began building a race car together. I was an associate pastor at the time. After awhile, I began to feel uncomfortable about it in my spirit, so I let it go. I explained to my friend, "I can't do this right now. The Lord won't let me." And I let him keep all the investment I had in the car.

Now, I'm not saying that the Lord is against our having a hobby, because He isn't. I'm simply saying that you need to obey His plan for your life, and if He leads you to give up some things in the process, you should do it. He may or may not ask you to give up something, but if He does, He will bless you if you obey Him.

It is human nature to want to make plans for your life, and that's not wrong. In fact, something would be wrong with someone who had no interest in having a plan for his or her life. You might have a plan, but the Lord might have *other* plans! That was true in my case.

Before Lynette and I were married, she had always said she would never marry a traveling minister. She wanted to be a pastor's wife. Well, when we married, I wasn't traveling. But later, God called me to begin traveling. That wasn't *my* plan; it was *His* plan. My dad was a traveling minister for most of my childhood, and I remembered the sacrifices we all had to make. And I didn't want to do it! I wanted to stay home and be with my family. But the Lord had other plans.

We traveled in ministry for a number of years, and Lynette even began to get used to it. She had accepted the fact that I was a traveling minister. But at about the same time she prayed and asked God to take away the desire to pastor, He said to us, "Now I want you to pastor."

To be honest, I really didn't want to pastor at first. I still had my own ideas about what I wanted to do in life. But I gave up my own plans and left them all behind to gain the satisfaction and the blessing of obeying God. I wanted God's best for our lives, and I knew that to receive that, as my father had, I had to follow in his footsteps of obedience to the Lord. I had to get in position to receive God's best through my obedience to Him.

Now, as I said before, there is a definite connection between obedience and faith. For example, a person could be obedient to God's specific will and plan for his life, but fail to obey His Word and lose out on the blessings. He could fail to use His faith in God's Word and allow himself to be robbed of many of the blessings of God that God intended he have.

On the other hand, a person could use his faith and believe God according to His Word, yet refuse to obey God in something God is speaking to him about, and God would be unable to bless his disobedience.

You see, you have to have both of them working together: obedience to God's *Word*, which is His will generally, and obedience to His *plan*, which is His specific will for you. When you get both of these working together, you will be in position to receive the blessings and glory of God.

---

[1] For in-depth accounts of Rev. Kenneth E. Hagin's experiences in life and ministry, see his book *I Believe in Visions*.

Chapter 10

DRAWING NEAR TO GOD

In the Bible, we see a direct correlation between people drawing near to God and His revealing His glory. God always responds to the heart that is hungry toward Him. James 4:8 says, "Draw near to God and He will draw near to you . . ." (*NKJV*).

We read it in a previous chapter, but let's look again at Leviticus chapter 9. Verse 5 says, "And they brought that which Moses commanded before the tabernacle of the congregation: and all the congregation DREW NEAR and stood before the Lord" (*KJV*).

Key Number Two: *Drawing Near to God*

We're looking at nine keys to experiencing God's greater glory. In the last chapter, we saw that key number one to experiencing the greater glory is *obedience*. Key number two is *drawing near to Him*.

You may be thinking, *What do you mean, 'Draw near to God'? I'm a Christian. I am in Christ. I'm already near Him.*

Well, that's true. *Positionally*, as believers, we are in Christ. We cannot draw any closer to God than we already are in Christ. But we can draw nearer to God *experientially*. We need to experience God in every area of our lives, and we need to draw near to Him and have fellowship with Him in our thoughts, our attitudes, and our worship.

JAMES 4:8 (NKJV)

8 Draw near to God and He will draw near to you . . . .

This verse is written to Christians, those who are in Christ and who have been brought near to God by Him (Eph. 2:13). Yet James 4:8 tells us that Christians can be closer to or further from God. And we know for ourselves that we can be closer to or further away from God in our thoughts, attitudes, and worship.

What does it mean, then, to draw near to God? It means that we commune with Him in our thoughts. It means we allow His Word to shape our attitudes in life, and we glorify Him in our lifestyle. It means that amidst the stress and pressures of everyday life, we take the time to focus on Him in our thought life. Our heart and mind are focused on Him, not on the affairs of life. We praise Him, truly grateful for who He is, what He's done for us, and what we have because of Him. Our worship is heartfelt and sincere.

The Difference Between Position and Experience

If we're not careful, our worship can become nothing more than a formality. The words of adoration that we speak or sing to Him can lose their meaning.

Have you ever been in the company of someone, and as you were talking to him or her, you noticed that the person wasn't really "there"? The person's thoughts were on something else, not on what you were saying. They were in your presence all right, yet they were "a thousand miles away" in their thoughts.

In other words, *positionally*, they were with you, but *experientially,* they were not. Well, as a Christian, you are *positionally* in God's Presence. You became joined to the Lord in the New Birth, and He lives in you, in your re-created spirit man.

How much closer to the Lord can you get than that? Well, *experientially*, you may not be living in close fellowship and communion with Him. You may not be spending time in His Word and in prayer. You may not be spending time just worshipping the Lord in all of His glory for His awesome goodness and love.

You see, there is a difference between position and experience! Positionally, you can't get any closer to God than you are right now if you are a Christian. But experientially, you can draw closer to Him.

Let me illustrate this fact to you another way. Let's say you were in a church service in which the Spirit of God was moving in a powerful way. Some were bowing in His Presence, just worshipping Him and fellowshipping with Him. Some were receiving the direction they'd been seeking or the answer to some question they'd been asking. For some, symptoms in their body were dissipating; they were receiving divine healing.

Others lay prostrate, repenting before Him as He prevailed upon them by His Spirit to surrender their whole heart to Him. Still others lay motionless in His Presence, unable to move, in awe of His holiness and majesty.

These people were experiencing something, weren't they! Now imagine others in that same building, working behind the scenes to help put on the meeting or service. They were working in housekeeping or in other areas, such as the nursery or children's areas. Positionally, they were in the building, but they weren't experiencing the same things the congregation was experiencing, because they weren't entering into the Presence of God. They were working; they weren't drawing near to God as the people in the service were drawing near to Him.

You see, our position in Christ entitles us to all the promises of God. But whether or not we actually receive those promises determines whether we'll experience and enjoy them.

Our Position Is Secure

Some believers aren't very certain about their position with God. They don't understand God's plan of redemption and the work Jesus accomplished on their behalf at the Cross of Calvary—in His death, burial, and resurrection. They often feel unworthy of drawing near to God. But the Bible says we can draw near to Him with full assurance of faith.

HEBREWS 10:22
22 Let us draw near to God with a sincere heart in full assurance of faith, having our hearts sprinkled to cleanse us from a guilty conscience and having our bodies washed with pure water.

It is through the blood of the Lord Jesus Christ that our hearts have been cleansed from the guilt caused by our sin nature. When we accept Jesus Christ as our Savior and Lord, that becomes our position: We are washed, cleansed by His blood, and made free to enjoy communion with the Most High. Our position changes from our being a part of the kingdom of darkness to having citizenship in the Kingdom of light! Positionally, we have been brought near to Him in a divine union. Now we must draw near to Him in our experience. We must enjoy fellowship with Him through His Word and through prayer.

We Must Draw Near With the Word

An experiential relationship is impossible apart from the Word of God. Romans 12:1 and 2 commands us to conform not to the world but to our new life in Christ through the renewing of our mind. So many Christians remain positionally united, but never go any further in their walk with God, because they never renew their mind with the Word. They never train their mind to think like God thinks—to think in line with His Word. They don't experience the blessings that others experience, and, unfortunately, over time, it becomes very easy for them to fall prey to worldly thinking and the enemy's lies, and they fall backward.

Others know a little about the Word, yet it seems they're always struggling. They're always striving where the blessings of God are concerned. Their lives seem to be speckled with a few blessings here and there. Now, I'm not saying these Christians are living in sin. Many of them are good people with good intentions. They live uprightly, but they're not seeking God and drawing near to Him through His Word, and they often succumb to the circumstances of life; they accept whatever life brings their way.

JOHN 15:7

7 If you remain in me and my words remain in you, ask whatever you wish, and it will be given you.

This verse is talking about experience! You can be a blood-bought, Heaven-bound, born-again child of God and still fail to abide in God's Word and allow it to abide or remain in you.

God Is Saying, 'Come Near'

Did you know that you can experience God in your everyday walk with Him? You can by renewing your mind to think as He thinks—by abiding in His holy written Word.

JAMES 4:8

8 Come near to God and he will come near to you . . . .

Some people live far from God in their thoughts, attitudes, and worship. They see Him as "distant" where their lives are concerned. But God says, "Come near"! God wants you to live close to Him in fellowship. He wants you to have that experience of living close to Him through the Word.

A Place of Protection

What are some of the experiences we can expect to have when we are drawing near to God? When you draw near to God, you will experience *a place of protection* in His Presence.

PSALM 91:1–4

1 He who dwells in the shelter of the Most High will rest in the shadow of the Almighty.

2 I will say of the Lord, "He is my refuge and my fortress, my God, in whom I trust."

3 Surely he will save you from the fowler's snare and from the deadly pestilence.

4 He will cover you with his feathers, and under his wings you will find refuge; his faithfulness will be your shield and rampart.

When I read these verses of Scripture, I think about my grandpa's farm back when I was a young boy. Pa Pa raised chickens, and I remember instances in which a hawk would fly overhead or a dog would come near the pen. Whenever the chickens were threatened in any way, the hens would begin clucking, as if calling to the chicks. The next thing you'd see was chicks running toward the hens. It seemed like as many as 10 or 12 at a time would squat down and get underneath those hens' wings and hide. Then there wouldn't be a chick in sight! They would all be hidden beneath the wings of those hens.

Similarly, when we run to God—when we draw near to Him—we find a place of protection under the shadow of the Almighty. We can hide in Him and be "covered with His feathers and find refuge under His wings" (Ps. 91:4).

I remember that anytime one of those young chicks on Pa Pa's farm was overtaken by a predator, it was when it was too far from its place of protection. When danger arose, the chick was too far away to find refuge in time to avert the danger.

In our Christian walk, though we became positionally in Christ in the New Birth, we can experientially get too far away from God's place of protection. We can allow distractions, the things of the world, offenses, and so forth to keep us far from the Father in our thoughts, attitudes, and worship. And, many times, needless tragedies that could have been avoided occur because a believer wasn't drawing near to God in his or her walk.

That's a hard thing to have to say, but it's true. We need to live close to God in fellowship daily, not just on Sunday or at a special meeting or seminar.

Now, I'm not saying that we have to stop all of our daily activity to pray continuously in order to remain in close fellowship with God. You can stay in an attitude of prayer *while* you're going about your daily affairs.

A *Lifestyle* of Prayer

Someone once asked my father how long he prayed each day. Years ago, it had become popular in some circles to pray and wait before the Lord one hour each day. The scriptures they were using were Matthew 26:40 and Mark 14:37, where Jesus had said to those with Him in the Garden of Gethsemane, "Could you not pray [or "watch"] with Me one hour?"

So someone inquired of my dad, asking him how much time he spent in prayer each day. You would be surprised how he answered the person.

First, let me say that my dad had some tremendous experiences with the Spirit of God in extended times of prayer and seeking the Lord. But he didn't pray like that every day.

Ephesians 6:18 says, "Praying always . . ." (*KJV*). Well, how are we going to do that? We can't just neglect our everyday responsibilities to sit around praying all the time. No, that's not what this verse is talking about.

As I said, you can be in an attitude of prayer constantly *at the same time* you're doing other things. That's what my dad did. If you were ever around him for very long, you'd know that he lived a lifestyle of prayer and fellowshipping with the Father. For example, Dad could be sitting in his recliner watching a football game on television and be totally into the game to the point of trying to help a player run the ball! Then there would be a lull in the game, and you could look over at Dad and find him praying in tongues under his breath. You'd see his lips moving, and if you got close enough, you could hear him praying quietly in the Spirit.

Dad lived experientially in a position of close fellowship with God. He knew what it meant to draw near to God continually and *live* near to God in his Christian walk. When that person asked Dad how much time he spent in prayer each day, Dad answered matter-of-factly: "Well, I *never* get out of fellowship with God." In other words, Dad led a *lifestyle* of prayer and fellowshipping with the Lord.

I can remember traveling with Dad to a revival meeting when I was about five years old. On the way, we stopped at Brother and Sister Goodwin's house to pray. Dad called them Mom and Dad Goodwin, and when Dad was out traveling, many times he would drive out of his way, sometimes hundreds of miles, just to stop by and pray with them for 20 or 30 minutes; he respected them that much.

On this particular visit to Mom and Dad Goodwin's house, they had finished praying, and we were just about to leave. In fact, we had left the house and had started down the walkway toward our car when Dad stopped and said, "We don't need to go just now. Let's go back inside and talk for little while."

So we went back inside. My mom and dad and Mom and Dad Goodwin drank a glass of iced tea and talked together. They weren't even talking about spiritual things; they were just chatting.

After about 15 minutes, Dad said, "Okay, we can go now."

So we got into our car, and as we got onto the highway, we drove up on a big wreck. A gasoline truck had overturned and was on fire. In fact, several cars were on fire. Dad asked someone standing on the side of the road when the accident happened.

"About fifteen minutes ago," the man said.

Dad turned to my mom and said, "If I hadn't obeyed God and stayed longer at the Goodwins', we would have been at this exact spot at the time of this wreck."

You see, when you're living close to God, in that place of protection, God can manifest Himself to keep you from harm. Too many times, the Holy Spirit tries to manifest Himself in believers' lives, warning them of something to come that they need to avoid. But they override that inward witness. They might say something, such as, "Oh, that's just me," and they miss out on a manifestation of the Spirit of God to bless and protect them.

A Place of Communion

If we're not living close to God, we won't be able to hear Him talking to us. He won't be able to manifest His Presence in our lives as He desires, because we're not drawing near to Him.

As I said, there are certain experiences we can expect to have when we are continually drawing near to God. We can experience a place of protection with Him, as we've already seen. We can also experience *a place of communion.*

Did you know that God desires intimate communion and fellowship with every one of us? But it's difficult to have an intimate conversation with someone if he or she is not close to you.

Have you ever tried to hold a conversation with someone who's standing far away? For example, have you ever tried to talk in detail to a person who was standing on the other side of a large room or building, or to a neighbor, perhaps, who was standing across the street?

If I was standing in my pulpit at RHEMA Bible Church and wanted to have a conversation, without a microphone, to one of my ushers standing in the back of the auditorium, it would be very difficult to do. I might try to holler, "How are you doing?" If he managed to hear me somehow, he might nod or give me a "thumbs up" signal, or he might even holler back, "I'm doing great!" But we couldn't really go beyond that and have an in-depth conversation, because we're standing too far away from one another.

In much the same way, if we're living too far away from God in our Christian walk—in our thoughts, attitude, and worship—we won't enjoy the privilege of communion with Him. And when a believer goes week after week, month after month, and even year after year without entering into that place of intimate communion with the Lord, his Christian experience will become lackluster and weak. That person could become so slack in his walk that he will succumb to every temptation and give in to every adverse circumstance that comes his way.

No More Temptation?

I've had people ask me, "How can I get away from temptation?"

As long as you're in this world, you won't get completely away from it ever. Now, certainly, you can exercise wisdom in keeping yourself out of the path of something you know will tempt you. But you can't get completely away from it, because temptation is the devil's *modus operandi* or "m.o." He uses temptation, or thoughts, feelings, and suggestions, to try to keep us from drawing near to God and to rob us of God's blessings.

So, as long as the devil is here on the earth, temptation will be here too. But if you want to learn how to overcome it, live experientially as close to God as you can. Refuse to let anything keep you from drawing near to Him and experiencing His manifest Presence in your life.

A Place of Receiving

We've looked at some of the experiences and blessings we can enjoy from God as we continually draw near to Him. When we draw near to Him, we can enter the place of experiencing His protection and communion. We can also enter into *a place of receiving* from Him.

Some people doubt the fact that God wants them to have all the blessings He has promised in His Word. God has made those blessings available to us, and He has told us about them in His Word. Those blessings were bought and paid for by the blood of the Lord Jesus Christ in His death, burial, and resurrection. So, since God paid for the blessings for us, why wouldn't He want us to have them!

Romans 8:32 says, *"He who did not spare his own Son, but gave him up for us all—how will he not also, along with him, graciously give us all things?"* If we are doubting the fact that God wants to bless us, we are not drawing near to Him. If we were drawing near to the Lord, fellowshipping with Him around His Word as we read, studied, and prayed, we would not be doubting His willingness to bless us. Instead of doubting, we would rejoice and receive that which He has provided.

The way to overcome doubt concerning the promises of God is through faith in the Word of God. How do you have faith in the Word? Romans 10:17 says, "So then faith cometh by hearing, and hearing by the word of God" (*KJV*).

It is easy to have faith in God's Word when we are drawing near to Him, fellowshipping with Him around His Word. The opposite is true too. When we are *not* drawing near to Him, we fall prey to doubt and unbelief because we haven't been hearing His Word as we should. We haven't been reading, studying, or meditating on the Word of God, and faith slips our grasp and eludes us.

God has made His will clear to us in the pages of His Word.

2 CORINTHIANS 1:20

**20 For no matter how many promises God has made, they are
"Yes" in Christ. And so through him the "Amen" is spoken
by us to the glory of God.**

This verse says that, in Christ, God is saying *yes* to every
promise He has made. But notice the last part of that verse:
"*. . . And so through him* [talking about Christ] *the "Amen"
is spoken by us. . . .*"

The literal meaning of that word "amen" is *so it is* or *so be
it*. While it is true that God has provided all these things for
us and has, through Christ, said "yes" to our receiving them,
we will never receive and enjoy these blessings unless we
add our faith to what God has said. In other words, unless
we add our "so be it" to God's "yes," we will never experience
the reality of these blessings in our lives!

'Must Be Present to Win'

We know it's true that God has provided all these blessings
for us. But you have to draw near to Him to receive them.
Another way to say it is like this: *"You must be present to win"*!

Have you ever entered a contest or drawing of some kind,
and one of the rules for receiving the prize was that you had
to be present to win? In other words, even if your name was
selected to win the prize, if you were not present at the time
of the drawing, you couldn't collect your winnings.

Well, spiritually speaking, your positional experience in
Christ *qualifies* you for the blessings of God, but it doesn't

guarantee you will actually be the recipient of the blessings and enjoy them for yourself. But as you draw near to God, you can appropriate them by faith and experience the manifest blessings of God! In other words, you must be present to win! Your positional experience in Christ *qualifies* you, but your "experiential" experience makes you the recipient!

Everyone is the winner, so to speak, when he accepts Jesus Christ as Savior and becomes born again. But we have to be present—we have to be experientially drawing near to God—in order to actually receive from Him. In that place of being near to the Father, we experience a place of protection, of communion, of receiving, and of enjoying *all* the blessings of God!

Chapter 11

THE ROLE OF THE INDIVIDUAL IN RECEIVING THE GLORY

In the last chapter, I talked about drawing near to God as one of the keys to experiencing His greater glory. Previously, we looked at Bible instances of God's glory, and saw that under the Old Covenant, the glory of God resided in the Temple. Then we saw that today, the Temple in which God resides is us, the Body of Christ.

In the New Covenant, God indwells *us. We are God's house!*

We also understand that the Body of Christ is made up of individuals, and God's Spirit also indwells each one of us individually. The Apostle Paul likened the Body of Christ to a natural body (1 Cor. 12:12,20), which consists of many members, such as eyes, ears, arms, hands, fingers, legs, feet, toes, and so forth. Each member or part of the body is important and has its place. Likewise, each member of Christ's Body is important and has his or her place.

In this chapter, I'm going to show you the importance of each believer taking his place in the Body of Christ, and his individual responsibility in receiving the greater glory.

We've established the fact that the Body of Christ is going to have to cooperate with God to usher in a move of His greater glory. But I think it's important to note that the Body of Christ can only do as a whole what individual members are doing. In other words, if individual members of the Body of Christ don't do their part to cooperate with this divine flow of God's glory, then the Body of Christ as a whole can't go forward in experiencing this great move of the Spirit of God.

Now, that's not to say that if a few members of the Body of Christ dig in their heels and refuse to go with this new move of God, every one of us will suffer. No, God is answering the cry of hungry hearts, and the heartfelt prayers of these saints of God will not be hindered by some who are unwilling, complacent, or even ignorant of what God wants to do in the earth.

Yet we as individual believers are going to have to get in position if we want to experience the greater glory. We can't be complacent, just sitting in our pews on Sunday morning, content with the status quo, and still expect to experience revival.

One Woman Who Took Responsibility and Rose Above Complacency

In the last chapter, I talked about the importance of drawing near to God. In James 4:8, which reads, "Draw near to God and He will draw near to you . . ." (*NKJV*), notice who is to take the first step. "You" is implied, isn't it? We could read it this way: "You draw near to God, and He will draw near to you."

It is *you* who is to do the drawing near to God. Let's look at a Bible example of someone who drew near to Jesus for herself.

MARK 5:25–34

25 And a woman was there who had been subject to bleeding for twelve years.

26 She had suffered a great deal under the care of many doctors and had spent all she had, yet instead of getting better she grew worse.

27 When she heard about Jesus, SHE CAME UP BEHIND HIM IN THE CROWD AND TOUCHED HIS CLOAK,

28 because she thought, "If I just touch his clothes, I will be healed."

29 Immediately her bleeding stopped and she felt in her body that she was freed from her suffering.

30 At once Jesus realized that power had gone out from him. He turned around in the crowd and asked, "Who touched my clothes?"

31 "You see the people crowding against you," his disciples answered, "and yet you can ask, 'Who touched me?' "

32 But Jesus kept looking around to see who had done it.

33 Then the woman, knowing what had happened to her, came and fell at his feet and, trembling with fear, told him the whole truth.

34 He said to her, "Daughter, your faith has healed you. Go in peace and be freed from your suffering."

First, let me say that this woman was an Israelite. She had a covenant with God, which entitled her to divine healing because healing was part of the covenant God had made with Abraham.

Yet notice that, although this woman had a covenant of healing, she was sick. And she *remained* sick until she took the responsibility to do something about it herself.

We've often heard it said, "Well, you never know what God is going to do."

But as a believer, if you live experientially close to Him, you know exactly what He's going to do! He's going to do just what His Word says He will do! That was the attitude of the woman with the issue of blood. After she heard about Jesus, she said to herself, ". . . *'If I just touch his clothes, I will be healed'* " (Mark 5:28).

Some people say, "Well, if God wants to heal me, He'll just do it."

But, no, they have a part to play, just as the woman with the issue of blood had a part to play.

What can we learn from the woman who had the issue of blood? One thing we can learn is that, she was determined to get in the presence of Jesus. And she did get to Him, at great risk to herself, because it was against her religion's practices to go out in public with an issue of blood. She risked the wrath of religious leaders and maybe even her peers.

There are many people today who aren't willing to risk anything to get in the Presence of God. For example, some people won't even go to church if it's raining too hard! Others will make the excuse, "That church is too big. I don't like

Who wants
do be at
a will reading
after boss of
a loved one

Jesus left
us His will
We are His heirs
Read Word
Will

crowds. I just want to attend a small church." (But, they're often not attending a small church, either!)

What if the woman with the issue of blood had had that attitude? What if she had said, "Well, I want to draw near to Jesus, but look at this crowd! It's going to be too hard to get close to Him"?

But, no, to get to Jesus, the woman started elbowing her way through the crowd. And I'm sure she was very weak in her condition, because the Bible says she'd had the disease for many years (Mark 5:25). She may even have had to *crawl* through that crowd to get to Jesus. But she got there! She didn't let anything stop her, yet it seems that some people will let anything stop them from pursuing God.

We know the end result of this woman's efforts and determination to get into the presence of Jesus. She received her healing, and she did it because she was willing to take responsibility for getting to Him—with no excuses and no holds barred!

We Need to 'Set Ourselves' to Seek Him

We all need to be more like the woman who had the issue of blood. We need to "set ourselves" and press in to receive from Him as she did. Isaiah 50:7 says, *"Because the Sovereign Lord helps me, I will not be disgraced. Therefore* have I set my face like flint, *and I know I will not be put to shame."* If we took this attitude in our prayer life, what wonders do you think would be wrought in our midst!

John Wesley is recorded as having said, "It seems God can do nothing in the earth unless someone asks Him." It is our responsibility individually as well as collectively, or corporately, to be sensitive to what God wants to do in the earth and then, in our praying and seeking Him, ask Him to do it!

Some people believe that if God wants to do something, He will just do it. They do not realize that we must cooperate with Him if He is going to manifest Himself in our midst as He desires. But God has always had those who sensed what He wanted to do in the earth and then set themselves to pray until it came to pass.

Teamwork in the Body of Christ

It will take each of us working together to experience a move of God's Spirit in the earth. God is not going to move just through ministers to reap the precious fruit, a harvest of souls, from the earth. He is going to use you and me—*all of us*—to do it.

Yet some have the mistaken idea that they are not important in the Body of Christ. Maybe they feel that because they don't minister behind a pulpit, they are less important than someone who does. But that couldn't be further from the truth! Every single one of us has a place. The Bible tells us so.

Read carefully the following passage from First Corinthians 12.

1 CORINTHIANS 12:13–27

13 For we were all baptized by one Spirit into one body— whether Jews or Greeks, slave or free—and we were all given the one Spirit to drink.

14 Now the body is not made up of one part but of many.

15 If the foot should say, "Because I am not a hand, I do not belong to the body," it would not for that reason cease to be part of the body.

16 And if the ear should say, "Because I am not an eye, I do not belong to the body," it would not for that reason cease to be part of the body.

17 If the whole body were an eye, where would the sense of hearing be? If the whole body were an ear, where would the sense of smell be?

18 But in fact God has arranged the parts in the body, every one of them, just as he wanted them to be.

19 If they were all one part, where would the body be?

20 As it is, there are many parts, but one body.

21 The eye cannot say to the hand, "I don't need you!" And the head cannot say to the feet, "I don't need you!"

22 On the contrary, those parts of the body that seem to be weaker are indispensable,

23 and the parts that we think are less honorable we treat with special honor. And the parts that are unpresentable are treated with special modesty,

24 while our presentable parts need no special treatment. But God has combined the members of the body and has given greater honor to the parts that lacked it,

25 so that there should be no division in the body, but that its parts should have equal concern for each other.

26 If one part suffers, every part suffers with it; if one part is honored, every part rejoices with it.

27 Now you are the body of Christ, AND EACH ONE OF YOU IS A PART OF IT.

Pay particular attention to verse 19, in which Paul writes, *"If they were all one part, where would the body be?"* He was saying that we all can't be the same. If we were all the same, we wouldn't be a Body.

No, each of us is unique, and each of us has his or her unique, individual function. That's why Paul wrote in verse 17, *"If the whole body were an eye, where would the sense of hearing be? If the whole body were an ear, where would the sense of smell be?"*

If you are having trouble seeing yourself as a valuable and precious member of the Body of Christ, you need to read and re-read these scriptures and meditate on them and other scriptures that tell you who you are in Christ. And you need to say to yourself, "I am a unique individual in the sight of God. In fact, I am so unique that no one else has the same plan for his or her life that God has for me."

In our natural body, we each have fingerprints that are unique to us; no one else in the world has fingerprints exactly like ours. Similarly, in the Body of Christ, each one of us is unique. Just as no two people have the same set of fingerprints, no two people in the Body of Christ have the same role or function. Yet how often do we needlessly compare ourselves to a fellow brother or sister in Christ? When we do that, we are forgetting that we are a unique creation of God and that each of us has his or her own unique place to fill in the Body.

Instead of filling their own place, many in the Body of Christ, are copying what someone else is doing. Now, stop and think about that for a minute. If you are trying to do what *someone else* is called to do, that means you are probably *not* doing what *you* are called to do!

Many pastors are struggling today because they are not doing what God specifically told them to do. Instead, they are trying to implement other pastors' church programs, and they are frustrated and unfulfilled.

"Well," someone said. "Some of these programs are good, and we need them in our churches."

If God says you need them, then you need them. But if He doesn't, let some other pastor implement those programs. Meanwhile, you be faithful to do what God called *you* to do.

Many have said to me, "Pastor Hagin, you need to start a Christian school."

I always say, "No, I don't!"

God didn't tell me to start a Christian school. He told us to start RHEMA Bible Training Center, and that takes up enough of our time and resources. We don't have the time to spend on something else that God hasn't told us to do.

I think this is where many pastors get into trouble. They allow people to pressure them into doing things that aren't part of the vision God gave them. Those things may be part of someone else's vision, but not theirs.

Some ministers succumb to the pressure because they think that if they don't, their church or ministry might lose money. Friend, I would rather lose money than get outside the vision that God has given me. It will cost you more in the long run, in more ways than one, if you let other people dictate to you the plan for your church or ministry.

Let us remember that we are a unique people for God! And God's plan for each of us is unique. We need each member to take his place and do what God called *him* to do, not what He has called someone else to do.

You are important and unique! When I'm teaching along these lines, I always emphasize that even the "little toe" in the Body of Christ is important to God and has his place!

Have you ever hurt your little toe? I have. I am one of those people who is a light sleeper and gets up at all hours of the night. I might get up to get a drink of water or check on our dogs or just to look outside.

I remember once I got up in the middle of the night and walked right into a chair that someone had moved. I was walking at a pretty good pace, too, because I know my way around my house at night. So I wasn't expecting to run into a chair that was where it wasn't supposed to be! And when my little toe caught the leg of that chair, let me tell you, my whole body felt the effect of it! I bent down and grabbed my foot and then hobbled along, trying to walk off the pain. (You can't walk without limping if you've hurt your toe—even your little toe.)

Well, spiritually speaking, doesn't the Bible say that when one member of the Body is hurt, the whole Body suffers (1 Cor.12:26)?

I hope you can see that each of us has a role and a responsibility in experiencing the greater glory in our midst. It will take each of us functioning in our place and working together to get the job done. And as we do it, we will reap a great harvest of souls for the Kingdom and be blessed in a greater measure individually and as a Body.

The Disappointment of Misplaced Expectancy

Besides functioning in his unique place, the individual believer has another responsibility, and that is to put his trust in God, not in man.

Some Christians attend a church service or meeting, and they expect the minister to somehow cause the Spirit of God to manifest in the meeting, as if that minister is supposed to "perform" for them. They aren't praying and believing God for that meeting. Their eyes aren't on Him, but on the minister. Their expectancy is misplaced, and that's why they are often disappointed with their experience.

Some ministers allow that misplaced expectation to pressure them. But they shouldn't. God gets all the glory when there is a move of the Spirit. The Holy Spirit manifests as He wills and upon whom He wills. God can use even a donkey if He wants to! He proved that in Numbers 22:3–35, where we read that the prophet Balaam's donkey spoke a word from the Lord to her master.

So, you see, if we are going to experience the greater glory in our midst, we have to get our eyes off people and on God.

He is where all the answers to life's problems lie. And He will not let us down!

Many Christians, even today, relegate the experience of God's Presence to ministers only. But God wants *all* of us to experience His Presence—and not just in church, but in our own personal lives.

JOHN 4:23,24 (KJV)

23 But the hour cometh, and now is, when the true worshippers shall worship the Father in spirit and in truth: for THE FATHER SEEKETH SUCH TO WORSHIP HIM.

24 God is a Spirit: and they that worship him must worship him in spirit and in truth.

Worship of God is something every Christian, not just ministers, should practice. And they should worship God continually, not just in church. These verses not only tell us that we *should* worship God, but they tell us *how* to worship Him: in Spirit and in truth.

Some people think that worshipping God in Spirit and in truth means worshipping Him by speaking in other tongues. Well, that is true to some degree; you can certainly worship the Lord in other tongues. But that is not the full intent of these verses.

Some say that John 4:23 and 24 is referring to having a godly, reverent attitude. This is true, too, but I think Jesus was also referring to the fact that worshipping God, who is a Spirit, would take place in the Spirit or in the Presence of God. In other words, to worship God in Spirit and in truth, you have to draw near to Him (James 4:8), as we saw in the last chapter.

Let me ask you a question. Do you have to wait to get to church to draw near to God? No, of course not. Now, I'm not negating the importance of church attendance and of attending special meetings and seminars. In fact, we are commanded not to forsake the assembling of ourselves together (Heb. 10:25). God anoints men and women to help usher people into the Presence of God in a powerful way wherein lives are touched and changed for His glory. But He is not limited to a meeting to manifest His Presence.

Your Relationship With God—Take It Personally

My dad taught for years the importance of having a personal relationship and walk with God. He taught countless numbers of people how to enter into God's Presence and fellowship with Him for themselves.

In my own life, I learned from my father the importance of having my own relationship with the Heavenly Father. You've probably heard me tell of the time I had trouble receiving healing of an ear disease at the age of 15. After much frustration, I learned that I had to receive healing from God for myself.

And I did receive my own healing from God. Dad wouldn't even pray for me that time, because I was old enough to do it for myself. He knelt beside me and agreed with me as *I* prayed. He said, "Son, *you* pray. I'm just going to 'scotch' for you." That meant he was going to agree with my faith and add his faith to mine, not exercise his faith *for* me without my putting forth any effort or using any faith for myself.

I believe that is what God is saying to us about our experiencing His Presence on a day-to-day basis. We have to draw near to Him in worship and learn to experience Him for ourselves!

The Presence of God resides in each of us as believers. But unless we are drawing near to Him and worshipping Him—fellowshipping with Him around His Word and in prayer—we will not be able to draw upon that divine Presence within.

I was preaching along this same line in a meeting, and the Lord led me to illustrate this point by having those present who had a checkbook with them to get it out and hold it in front of them.

I addressed them, "Do you understand that if you have money in your checking account, you are *right now* in the presence of money?" But unless you actually write a check or make a transaction, that money is not going to do you any good!

Similarly, you can be in the Presence of God, but His Presence will not affect you and bless, help, or change you unless you draw upon that Presence.

And you can draw upon the Presence of God at any time and at any place—while you're driving your car, while you're at home or on the job, when you're in the emergency room at a hospital, or facing some other critical need.

I draw on the Presence of God every day! Every morning when I get out of bed, I say to the Lord, "This is the day that You have made; I will rejoice and be glad in it [Ps. 118:24]. I draw upon Your wisdom today, Lord. As I face situations today that require decisions, Your wisdom will guide and instruct me. Thank You for your divine wisdom."

I could not do what I do as the president and executive operating officer of Kenneth Hagin Ministries without tapping into the Presence of God to help me. And I encourage you to draw from God's Presence on *your* job. As you do, He will give you wisdom beyond your education and your years. He'll show you how to do things that even your superiors can't do!

I have heard story after story about believers who were promoted on their jobs to positions that required degrees or certain experience that they did not have. But because they knew how to draw upon God's Presence, God gave them the wisdom and understanding they needed to perform in an extraordinary way.

Some people, even those who have been saved for years, believe that church is the only place you can draw from the Presence of God. They have not realized the blessings and benefits that come from drawing upon His Presence continually in everyday life.

We Were Created to Fellowship With God

God desires that you walk in and experience His divine Presence, and He doesn't want you to do it just when you're in church. God created man with the ability to experience His Presence individually, or one-on-one. Beginning with Adam and Eve, mankind was created to experience and walk in the Presence of God. It was only after Adam and Eve sinned that they broke fellowship with the Creator and ran from His Presence.

GENESIS 3:8 (NKJV)

8 And they heard the sound of the Lord God walking in the garden in the cool of the day, and Adam and his wife hid themselves from the presence of the Lord God among the trees of the garden.

This is the first time in the Bible that the Presence of God is actually mentioned, but we know that before they fell from grace, Adam and Eve were accustomed to fellowshipping with God.

Man was created to fellowship with God Almighty. And that is what Adam and Eve did until they fell from grace through sin and disobedience. At that point, instead of meeting God in the garden in the cool of the day, they were hiding from the Presence of God.

Have you ever noticed today that when a Christian is walking in a backslidden state and is doing things he shouldn't be doing (as well as *not* doing things that he *should* be doing), he usually avoids being in the presence of other Christians who are walking closely with God?

Sin avoids the very Presence of God because God's Presence convicts the person of his or her sin. God condemns sin—He cannot look upon sin—but He doesn't condemn the sinning one. He sent Jesus to die in our place for sin. And through Him, no matter how badly we may have missed it, we can be reconciled to God.

2 CORINTHIANS 5:19,20

19 God was reconciling the world to himself in Christ, NOT COUNTING MEN'S SINS AGAINST THEM. And he has committed to us the message of reconciliation.

20 We are therefore Christ's ambassadors, as though God were making his appeal through us. We implore you on Christ's behalf: BE RECONCILED TO GOD.

These verses are talking about God's reconciling the world—the unsaved—to Himself through Christ's redemptive work. When you become a Christian, or when you are reconciled to God, you become one of His very own children. Well, since God sent Jesus to reconcile us to Himself when we were sinners, how much more do you think He wants you to be reconciled to Him if you miss it and sin *after* you become His child! Because of Jesus' redemptive work and the great mercy and longsuffering of the Father, you can have fellowship restored that has been broken through sin.

As I said, often Christians who are backslidden feel uncomfortable and uneasy around Christians who are walking with God and experiencing His Presence. But God doesn't want those who have missed it to run *from* His Presence; He wants them to run *to* Him and be restored so that they can once again experience His blessed Presence.

Notice that sin separated Adam and Eve from the Presence of God, and it is sin that separates us from His Presence today. But think about the magnitude of God's great love! From the moment Adam and Eve sinned and became separated from God, He began setting in motion His plan to restore man to a place of experiencing and enjoying His Presence.

We need to realize that we were created to experience the glory of God. God desires that we learn to walk and live in His Presence for ourselves individually as well as corporately. As each of us learns to draw upon His Presence for ourselves, great things will begin to happen when we come together, and we will see greater and greater manifestations of God's glory in our midst.

Chapter 12

CONSECRATION AND UNITY
Two Catalysts to Glory

In Chapters 9 through 15, we're studying nine keys to experiencing God's greater glory. In chapters 9 and 10, we learned that obeying God and drawing near to God are two ways we can tap into the Presence of God and experience His greater glory.

In this chapter, we're going to look at consecration and unity as ways to experience more of God's glory.

2 CHRONICLES 5:11,13,14

11 The priests then withdrew from the Holy Place. All the priests who were there had **CONSECRATED THEMSELVES**, regardless of their divisions.

13 The trumpeters and singers joined in unison, as with one voice, to give praise and thanks to the Lord. Accompanied by trumpets, cymbals and other instruments, they raised their voices in praise to the Lord and sang: "He is good; his love endures forever." Then the temple of the Lord was filled with a cloud,

14 and the priests could not perform their service because of the cloud, for **THE GLORY OF THE LORD FILLED THE TEMPLE OF GOD.**

Notice that everyone who took part in the ceremonial worship of God consecrated themselves. Someone asked, "Well, how does that apply to us today?" If we want to see the greater glory, we must dedicate ourselves to God. We must commit ourselves to doing the will of God. We must pray and mean it from our heart, "Not my will, Lord, but Yours be done."

Key Number Three: *Consecration*

Key number three to experiencing God's glory is *consecration*. When you pray, "Not my will, but Yours," or "If it be Thy will," you are praying the prayer of consecration and dedication. Someone might ask, "I thought you weren't supposed to pray, 'If it be Thy will' if you're walking by faith."

Well, if you're praying the prayer of faith for something the Bible already says you can have, then there is no need to add, "If it be Thy will" to your prayer. For example, the Bible makes plain the fact that Jesus purchased our healing in His death, burial, and resurrection. First Peter 2:24 says, "*. . . by his wounds you have been healed.*" Therefore, you wouldn't need to pray, "If it be Thy will" when praying for healing, because God has already made His will known concerning healing.

But there are areas in which you don't know the will of God, such as praying about which job to take or about moving to a different location. You'd have to pray and seek God to determine His will for you in those cases, and you would have to pray, "If it be Thy will" or "Thy will be done."

Just because you're walking by faith doesn't mean you don't have to pray the prayer of consecration and dedication to God! No, in fact, just the opposite is true. If you have faith in God, you should *want* to do His will. You should have the attitude, "Lord, I will lay aside *my* plans and everything that *I* want to do. I only want to do what *You* want me to do." That's not always easy to do. But we must do it if we want God's best in life—His richest blessings and His greater glory.

As I said in the last chapter, pastors need to lay aside their own programs and plans and get *God's* plan for their church. A man's program is not going to fill the church. But God's plan will. Jesus said, ". . . if I be lifted up from the earth, I will draw all men unto me" (John 12:32 *KJV*). We have to choose God's plans over our own plans.

Now I'm not saying that church programs are wrong in themselves. We have many programs in our church to help people in the natural. But programs aren't necessarily going to draw people. Programs don't bring the greater glory. It's lifting up Jesus that will bring the greater glory.

In his ministry, John the Baptist said, concerning Jesus, "He must increase, but I must decrease" (John 3:30 *KJV*). That should be our attitude too. We should want to have Jesus exalted in our life and ministry, not ourselves. When we exalt Him, the King of kings and Lord of lords, we will experience greater manifestations of the glory of God.

Key Number Four: *Walking in Unity Before God*

Key number four to experiencing God's greater glory is *walking in unity before God.*

Let's look again at our passage in Second Chronicles chapter 5.

2 CHRONICLES 5:11,13,14

11 The priests then withdrew from the Holy Place. All the priests who were there had consecrated themselves, regardless of their divisions.

13 The trumpeters and singers JOINED IN UNISON, AS WITH ONE VOICE, to give praise and thanks to the Lord. Accompanied by trumpets, cymbals and other instruments, they raised their voices in praise to the Lord and sang: "He is good; his love endures forever."

Then the temple of the Lord was filled with a cloud,

14 and the priests could not perform their service because of the cloud, for the glory of the Lord filled the temple of God.

Notice this passage says that priests and musicians were assembled together, and both groups had their assignments. There were also those who took care of the building and the implements used in the ceremonies—the instruments of worship. The point I want to make is that each one did his part and fulfilled his own assignment.

Now notice again verse 13 of Second Chronicles 5.

2 CHRONICLES 5:13

13 The trumpeters and singers JOINED IN UNISON, AS WITH ONE VOICE, to give praise and thanks to the Lord. Accompanied by trumpets, cymbals and other instruments, they raised their voices in praise to the Lord and sang: "He is good; his love endures forever."

THEN THE TEMPLE OF THE LORD WAS FILLED WITH A CLOUD.

Unity is a vital key to God manifesting His glory, and we can see that throughout the Scriptures. It is no less true in our day. If we are going to see greater and greater manifestations of God's glory, we're going to have to walk in unity with other members of the Body, with our brothers and sisters in Christ.

When I talk about unity, I'm not just talking about being in unity with Christians in your church or in your camp— your particular denomination or group. (However, you certainly do need to be in unity with your fellow church members!) We *all* need to come together in unity, walking in love toward one another and esteeming each believer as a valuable member of the Body. There is strength in numbers, especially when unity exists among those numbers!

Those who follow and support our ministry (and I'm talking about every one of them, whether or not they are a graduate of the training center and whether or not they are in full-time ministry) are a part of this ministry. They are partners whom God has joined with us to help us do our part in this last-day revival on the earth. And we, along with others in the Body of Christ, are going to help usher in the latter rain and the great harvest of souls—the precious fruit of the earth—and the soon return of Jesus Christ. But, as I said, even in our own camps, we must demonstrate *greater unity* if we're going to experience *greater glory*.

Let's look at just a couple of New Testament instances in which God poured out His Spirit when the people were in unity.

ACTS 2:1–4 (KJV)

1 And when the day of Pentecost was fully come, they were all WITH ONE ACCORD in one place.

2 And suddenly there came a sound from heaven as of a rushing mighty wind, and it filled all the house where they were sitting.

3 And there appeared unto them cloven tongues like as of fire, and it sat upon each of them.

4 And they were all filled with the Holy Ghost, and began to speak with other tongues, as the Spirit gave them utterance.

This passage describes the Day of Pentecost. After the believers assembled together in unity—"with one accord"—they heard what sounded like a mighty wind blowing, which filled the house, and they saw what looked like fire, which "sat" upon each of them. Then they were filled with the Holy Ghost and spoke with other tongues.

After this instance, in Acts 3:1–8, we can read the account of the lame man healed at the gate called Beautiful as Peter and John were entering the temple. After the man was healed, there was an uproar among the priests and the Sadducees, who persecuted and then threatened Peter and John if they preached or taught further in the Name of Jesus Christ.

What did Peter and John do? Acts 4:23 says, "And being let go, THEY WENT TO THEIR OWN COMPANY, and reported all that the chief priests and elders had said unto them" (*KJV*).

You know, there's no place in the world like "your own company." There's nothing like being around those of like-precious faith.

Let's look at what happened when Peter and John went to their own company.

ACTS 4:23,24,29–31 (KJV)

23 And being let go, they went to their own company, and reported all that the chief priests and elders had said unto them.

24 And when they heard that, they lifted up their voice to God WITH ONE ACCORD, and said, Lord, thou art God, which hast made heaven, and earth, and the sea, and all that in them is:

29 And now, Lord, behold their threatenings: and grant unto thy servants, that with all boldness they may speak thy word,

30 By stretching forth thine hand to heal; and that signs and wonders may be done by the name of thy holy child Jesus.

31 And when they had prayed, the place was shaken where they were assembled together; and they were all filled with the Holy Ghost, and they spake the word of God with boldness.

When Peter and John got in the presence of their fellow believers, they all began to pray together in unity. And verse 31 says: ". . . the place was shaken . . . they were all filled with the Holy Ghost, and they spake the word of God with boldness."

The Holy Spirit was manifested when the people prayed together in unity! And, today, it's going to take all of us in the Body of Christ working with—not against—each other in prayer, in faith, and in fellowship to get the job done that God wants accomplished in this day.

A minister of a certain Pentecostal denomination once asked me, "How are your RHEMA graduates and RHEMA churches able to accomplish so much?"

I said, "Well, for one thing, we are simply obeying and carrying out the vision that God gave us [and you *should* be experiencing success if you are fulfilling God's plan for your life in His timing]. Another thing is, we are all working together toward a common goal. We all have the same vision, and we're working together in unity to fulfill the vision. We're not competing with one another; we're working *with* one another."

Years ago, I counseled one graduate who was a pastor in a certain city. He was bitter because another RHEMA graduate had come to his city and started a church. I asked the disgruntled pastor, "How many people do you have in your church?"

He replied, "About three hundred."

"Well, how big is this city?" I asked.

He said, "Well, there's about fifty thousand people here."

I responded, "You know, there are a lot of people in this city who are not members of your church! I don't think that other guy is going to take anything away from you by starting another work. Besides, his church is on the other side of town. You should be glad to have another Full Gospel church in the city."

Strife Is a Thief That Will Rob You of the Blessings of God

I later discovered that this pastor was upset because he wasn't unique any more from the standpoint of being the only RHEMA pastor in town. He had gotten distracted by what someone else was doing, and he wasn't thinking clearly. He lost focus of what God had called him to do because he got out of unity with a fellow minister.

Getting into strife will hinder you from receiving manifestations of the Presence of God in your life and ministry. James 3:16 says, "For where envying and strife is, there is confusion and every evil work" (*KJV*). Where there is strife, the Presence of God will not be in manifestation, because the Bible says that confusion and every evil work will be in manifestation instead.

The Power of Holding Steady When Things Seem to Go Wrong

When I first began traveling with my father as his crusade director, I didn't have very many meetings of my own. I had left full-time ministry as an associate pastor to become a crusade director. It looked as if I was taking a step backward. But God said to do it, so I did it.

As far as my responsibilities as crusade director went, I had no preaching duties whatsoever! It was months before I preached again.

During those long months, I had many opportunities at meetings and conventions to meet pastors and other ministers. Some of these pastors were scheduling meetings with fellows I knew from Bible school who, in my estimation, couldn't preach their way out of a paper bag! Many of these pastors knew that I was available to preach, but it seemed I couldn't get a meeting.

Sometimes the reason why some ministers are not promoted in their ministries is, they are not willing to stay faithful in the hard places. They want to "go" even if God is saying, "Hold steady."

Philip is one example of someone who had preached to large crowds and then found himself, in obedience to the Spirit of God, ministering in the desert to only one man. But Philip was faithful to obey, not leaning to his own understanding, and I believe that's why God was able to use him the way He did.

In Acts chapter 8, Philip is going down to the city of Samaria to preach. Let's look at what happened when he preached Christ to the people there.

ACTS 8:6–8 (KJV)

6 And the people **WITH ONE ACCORD** gave heed unto those things which Philip spake, hearing and seeing the miracles which he did.

7 For unclean spirits, crying with loud voice, came out of many that were possessed with them: and many taken with palsies, and that were lame, were healed.

8 And there was great joy in that city.

Notice the people were "with one accord" in giving heed to the things Philip was preaching. And signs and wonders followed the preaching of the Gospel, because we read that the people "heard and saw" the miracles God wrought by him (v. 6). Many were delivered from devils and demon possession, and others were healed who were sick in their bodies. And it says there was great joy in that city as a result.

Philip had a time in that city, didn't he? Then verse 26 says that the angel of the Lord called him away to the desert, where he ministered to a dignitary who was just sitting there in his chariot reading after the prophet Isaiah. Philip explained the One Isaiah was prophesying about, preached Jesus unto the man, and the man became born again and was water baptized (vv. 27–38).

Afterward, the Spirit of the Lord "caught away," or translated, Philip and took him to another city where he continued to preach Christ there and in other cities (vv. 39,40). But you have to understand that Philip's preaching to hundreds, thousands, or to one man was all in obedience to the Lord, not just according to what Philip wanted to do.

I can honestly tell you that when I first began serving as crusade director for my dad, I felt as if I was out in the desert somewhere, much like Philip was when he ministered to just that one man. But, like Philip, I knew that I was following the leading of the Lord. So I stayed steady.

It wasn't always easy for me to stay steady, especially when these pastors who were inviting my friends to hold meetings knew that I was available too. But before long, I began doing more and more preaching, including preaching to a crowd of approximately 10,000 in South Africa. I also preached at some Full Gospel Businessmen's events, and, eventually, began to have some notoriety from the standpoint that I was being invited to more meetings than I could accept.

One day, I finally did receive an invitation from one of the more well-known pastors who had overlooked me for a meeting just a few years before. He said, "I need you to come to my church. You could really help me."

I would be dishonest if I said that I didn't feel my blood about to boil as this pastor approached me about a meeting! I could have answered him, "Well, where were *you* when I needed *you*?" But my namesake had taught me differently, so I quietly said to the man, "Sure. If the Lord tells me to come, I'll come."

And I meant it! If God had led me to preach in that man's church, I would have gone, and I would have done it willingly and with a good attitude. But I wouldn't have been able to have that kind of attitude if I hadn't learned to stay put when God wanted me to stay put. You see, when you know God is leading you, you can endure a few hard times, because you know the future is bright. As my dad always said, "Preparation time is never wasted time." You may feel as though you're wasting time during certain seasons in your life. But if you're waiting on God, being faithful to His Word, and obeying Him where you're at, "payday" will come!

Walking in Love Doesn't Cost You—It *Pays!*

It pays to walk in an attitude of unity and love. In fact, you only hinder yourself when you're not walking in love and you're focusing on the wrong someone has done to you.

Now I'm not saying that just because I made it through that difficult time that I am never tempted to get into strife. As I said before, as long as we're on this earth, we will never get away from temptation. In fact, it hasn't been too long ago that someone said some unkind things about my dad and me and the ministry, calling all of us by name. I could have easily yielded to the flesh and got into strife about that minister! But I prayed, "Lord, forgive him. He doesn't know what he's talking about. Forgive him and bless him, Lord."

I have too many scars on my hands that I received in my younger days by acting in haste when others wronged me or a member of my family! Certainly, I think there are times when everyone wants to call someone who's wronged him and invite that person over to lunch for a "knuckle sandwich"! That may be what you feel like doing, but, thank God, we have the power to walk in love and unity and keep strife out of our lives so that we can have fellowship with God and experience His blessings.

People have written entire books about this ministry, criticizing us about things that were untrue. They have taken things Dad has said out of context and twisted them to mean something Dad never actually said, believed, or intended. We never responded or retaliated because we knew it would cost us something with God if we did, and it was a price we didn't want to pay.

My dad always said, "When others wrong you, don't get down and wallow in the mud with them. Stay on the high road."

Reading some of the instances connected with the Early Church should inspire us to want to walk in unity as never before. So what are we going to do? Are we going to have the attitude, "Well, that group doesn't believe like we do. We don't need them, anyway"? Or are we going to embrace *every* member of the Body of Christ, all those who have been born again by the blood of the Lord Jesus Christ?

We all might not believe exactly the same way, and there will always be some differences among us. But how we conduct ourselves will largely determine whether we'll experience the glory of God in a greater measure than we've seen up till now. If we dedicate ourselves to doing the will of God, including His will that we walk in love and unity, I believe we will see what the Early Church witnessed of the move of the Spirit of God, and *greater* things will we see in the days to come!

Chapter 13

GOD'S GLORY
IN OUR WORSHIP

In this chapter, we'll look at thanksgiving, praise, and worship as keys to experiencing God's greater glory. But before I go on, I want to emphasize that the nine keys that I'm sharing in these few chapters are not intended as a list of "dos" or of works that we are to perform in an effort to somehow manipulate the moving of the Spirit. They are intended as something that we are to embrace as a lifestyle.

In other words, the giving of thanks and praise to God is not something we're supposed to do now and then when we think about it or when we read a good book or hear a good sermon on the subject. God desires that we develop in the practice of praise and thanksgiving so that they flow from our hearts to Him. He wants us to praise and worship Him, not just for what He can do for us—or so that we can get something from Him—but because we love Him. (And the more we know about the Lord, the more we do love Him.)

In this chapter, I'm going to talk about our thanks, praise, and worship of God as attitudes of the heart that will position us to experience greater and greater measures of His glory in our midst.

Key Number Five: *Giving Thanks to God*

Key number five to experiencing the greater glory is *giving thanks to God.*

EPHESIANS 5:18–20 (KJV)

18 And be not drunk with wine, wherein is excess; but be filled with the Spirit;

19 Speaking to yourselves in psalms and hymns and spiritual songs, singing and making melody in your heart to the Lord;

20 GIVING THANKS ALWAYS for all things unto God and the Father in the name of our Lord Jesus Christ.

Notice in verse 18, Paul said, ". . . Be filled with the Spirit." We must maintain a Spirit-filled life if we are going to see the greater glory.

Then notice that in the following verse, Paul told the Church at Ephesus—and it applies to all of us—how to maintain the Spirit-filled life: "Speaking to yourselves in psalms and hymns and spiritual songs, singing and making melody in your heart to the Lord."

Then Paul said something else in connection with the Spirit-filled life: "GIVING THANKS ALWAYS for all things . . . in the name of our Lord Jesus Christ" (v. 20 *KJV*). Giving thanks is a means of maintaining a Spirit-filled life and positioning ourselves to receive of God's glory.

Now this verse, "Giving thanks always for everything" doesn't mean we are to thank God for everything that happens from the standpoint of believing that He is the author of it and that we should show appreciation for some sickness or disease, for example, that we are dealing with. No, God is not the author of sickness and disease. We don't thank Him *for* sickness, disease, or other adversity or tragedy. We thank Him *in* these things—in the midst of them—because He is able to deliver us out of them all (1 Thess. 5:18 *KJV*; Ps. 34:19)!

Let's look at a familiar Old Testament passage that connects the giving of thanks with God's glory.

2 CHRONICLES 5:13,14

13 The trumpeters and singers joined in unison, as with one voice, to give PRAISE AND THANKS to the Lord. Accompanied by trumpets, cymbals and other instruments, they raised their voices in praise to the Lord and sang: "He is good; his love endures forever." Then the temple of the Lord was filled with a cloud,

14 and the priests could not perform their service because of the cloud, for the glory of the Lord filled the temple of God.

Verse 13 says that when these musicians and singers joined in unity to give praise and thanks to the Lord, ". . . the temple of the Lord was filled with a cloud."

We know that the cloud that filled the Temple was the glory of God, because the next verse tells us, ". . . the priests could not perform their service because of the cloud, for *the glory of the Lord* filled the temple . . . ."

Why do we need to practice a lifestyle of thanksgiving today? So that we can maintain a Spirit-filled life—so that the glory of the Lord can continually fill us, His temple!

When we give thanks to God continually, we develop the habit of thankfulness in our lives, or what some call an "attitude of gratitude." Then, because we have practiced thanksgiving as a lifestyle, we are ready when the pressures of life come our way. When the pressures come to "squeeze" us, instead of yielding to fear, doubt, and unbelief, thanksgiving will come oozing out of us like water from a sponge! We will be able to give praise and thanks to God, saying, "The Lord is good, and His mercy endures forever"!

To illustrate the importance of giving thanks to God, I sometimes tell a story about two angels sent out from God who supposedly visited the earth every morning. As the story goes, both angels carried baskets as they walked throughout the earth. One of the angels had a basket to collect requests, and the other one had a basket to collect praise and the giving of thanks.

In a short time, the basket of requests was full and running over. But at the end of the day, the angel with the "praise-and-thanks" basket had only a mere two or three thank-yous.

Of course, that is just a story, but the principle is a good one. Although we don't find in Scripture angels carrying baskets to and from the earth, the story illustrates that

Christians can oftentimes be long on requests, but a little short on gratitude and the giving of thanks.

Key Number Six: *Giving Praise to God*

Key number six to experiencing God's greater glory is closely related to key number five, and that is *giving praise to Him.*

One of the most graphic New Testament accounts of God manifesting His power to deliver someone in a spectacular way was the one concerning Paul and Silas as they suffered torture and faced the possibility of death in prison, where they were incarcerated for preaching the Gospel (*see* Acts 16:16–34).

ACTS 16:23–26 (KJV)

23 And when they had laid many stripes upon them [Paul and Silas], **they cast them into prison, charging the jailor to keep them safely:**

24 Who, having received such a charge, thrust them into the inner prison, and made their feet fast in the stocks.

25 And at midnight Paul and Silas prayed, and sang PRAISES unto God: and the prisoners heard them.

26 And suddenly there was a great earthquake, so that the foundations of the prison were shaken: and immediately all the doors were opened, and every one's bands were loosed.

Verse 25 says, ". . . at midnight Paul and Silas prayed, and sang praises unto God . . . ." I want to point out something very interesting about the conditions these men found themselves in when they began to lift their voices in praise to God. It was midnight, and Paul and Silas were bound, with their feet in stocks, in the innermost part of that prison. They weren't at some special meeting with instruments and musicians, where everyone was waving their hands in the air and shouting, "Glory!" No, it wasn't a happy time. It wasn't a time of celebration concerning their circumstances.

And in our own lives, it's not just during the happy moments in life that we are to praise the Lord. In fact, it's often in our darkest hour—our "midnight" hour—that we need to praise Him the most.

What happened when Paul and Silas began to pray and sing praises to God in the midnight hour in that prison? It says, ". . . suddenly there was a great earthquake, so that the foundations of the prison were shaken: and immediately all the doors were opened, and every one's bands were loosed" (v. 26)!

What brought God's power, the glory of God, on the scene to deliver these men in their darkest hour? It was *their praise of Him.*

The Lord once said to me, "People are not missing it in their believing; they're missing it in their praise."

I immediately understood what the Lord was saying. Most of us know what the Word says. We know how to confess the Word. But when the pressure is on, and our back is against the wall, are we going to cower in fear and buckle under the pressure? Or are we going to lift our hands in praise to Him Who is faithful?

I'm not talking about going through the motions of praise. When I talk about praising the Lord, I'm talking about doing something that comes from the heart, something that causes you to lift your hands or fall to your knees in gratitude and in awe of God Himself.

ACTS 16:25,26 (KJV)

25 And at midnight Paul and Silas prayed, and sang praises unto God: and the prisoners heard them.

26 And suddenly there was a great earthquake, so that the foundations of the prison were shaken: and immediately all the doors were opened, and every one's bands were loosed.

It was a move of the Spirit of God that caused that prison to be shaken at its foundations so that every door flew open and everyone's bands, or chains, were loosed. And two men's heartfelt praise of God was the key to experiencing that spectacular move of the Spirit and glory of God.

Key Number Seven: *Worshipping God*

Key number seven to experiencing the greater glory is *worshipping God*. The Bible says that God seeks out those who will worship Him (John 4:23). God delights in manifesting Himself when people are worshipping Him from the depths of their heart for who He is, for His awesome greatness.

If you look at the Body of Christ today, you will find that worship is returning to the house of God. I'm talking about true worship, not entertainment, show, or just focusing on what God can do for us and on having a good time at church. I'm talking about a true reverence for a holy and loving God who has broken the barrier separating man from Himself through the Person of Jesus Christ.

It is good that we are getting back to a true worship of God that comes from our heart, not just from our head. The attitude of our heart and our priorities and focus are what will determine whether we enter into God's greater glory.

In our church, we have seen a greater move of the Spirit of God as a result of our renewed focus on worship. At times, our congregation just spontaneously erupts in worship and praise. No one tells them to do it. Our song leader and musicians don't lead them to do it. They are simply drawing near to God with their whole heart, and we are experiencing some powerful moves of the Spirit as a result.

Also, some time ago, we began holding Sunday evening "Prayer and Praise" services every fourth Sunday of the month. You might expect that people wouldn't attend a service like this as faithfully as a regular or traditional church service. But that's not the case at our church! Our members fill the auditorium, and we always have a tremendous time of prayer, praise, and worship. There is no preaching or teaching. My wife may exhort the people for a few minutes, and then we pray. Afterward, we always have a time of praise and worship. Our musicians play their instruments, and you can sense the glory of God in that auditorium in a powerful way.

Even while we are praying, our musicians play their instruments softly. And as the anointing comes upon them at times, they will begin playing to a crescendo. Then they will go back to playing softly. There is an ebb and flow of the anointing in the services.

Sometimes, spiritual songs will come forth as we are praising and worshipping God. And at times, everyone present will spontaneously kneel down in worship under the anointing of the Spirit. Once, more than an hour after we were supposed to be dismissed, everyone in the auditorium was lying prostrate on the floor with no one moving around or speaking a word. We were silent before the Lord, in awe of His power and majesty.

If there is going to be a move of the Spirit of God in the Body of Christ, our focus must be on the worship of Him. If we're going to usher in a tremendous move of the Spirit, we're going to have to learn to praise and worship Him from our hearts, in Spirit and in truth. We can't just praise the Lord from our minds and be content in our services with doing a little "bunny hop" dance in time with the music!

That's not true praise and worship, and it won't produce a true move of the Spirit of God. But I truly believe that as we embrace as a lifestyle these keys of giving thanks, praise, and worship to God, we will move closer to experiencing a move of the Spirit in our midst such as we've never seen before.

Chapter 14

PRAYING OUR WAY TO GREATER GLORY

Prayer is a very important Bible subject that we *must* understand if we are to cooperate with the plan of God for our lives and with His plan in the earth. Earlier, I quoted John Wesley as saying that it seems God can do nothing in the earth unless someone asks Him. God *wants* us to us ask of Him! God desires that we make requests and supplications on our behalf and on behalf of others. And He especially wants us to ask of Him where His will and plans and purposes are concerned.

Prayer is our means of communication with the Father. And He has given us the authority in Jesus' Name to pray. In fact, it is not only our God-given *privilege* and *right*, it is our *responsibility* as believers to be people of prayer.

Key Number Eight: *Prayer*

Key number eight to experiencing God's greater glory is *prayer*. And when I say "prayer," I'm talking about real, heartfelt prayer that gets results!

Growing up in the home of a preacher, even as a young boy, I remember attending prayer meetings in which people actually prayed! I mean, they got down on their knees and made heartfelt requests and supplications to God. They knew how to pray and how to receive real results from their praying.

In more recent times, I've been in other prayer meetings and seen people just sitting in their seats reading the Bible. But the reason it's called a prayer meeting is because you're supposed to *pray*, not have a time of Bible reading!

I am in no way saying it's wrong to read the Bible. In fact you might need to look up a specific verse to establish that your prayer is in line with God's will. But you have to understand that when it's time for prayer—whether it's a time of personal prayer or a prayer meeting—we need to pray!

Bible Prayer Reaps Bible Results!

Most people will pray to God when they're facing a crisis of some kind. Even the unsaved will seek divine help in time of trouble. And for so many, prayer is something they do blindly in that they pray without having Bible knowledge about *how* to pray. As a result, their prayers are "hit and miss."

In other words, sometimes they obtain a favorable result, and sometimes they don't. It's such a hit-and-miss proposition with them, sometimes they even take the attitude regarding their praying, "Well, you win some, and you lose some."

But Bible prayer will always reap Bible results! If we pray according to the Word, we will receive the results the Word promises. Therefore, once we come to understand that it is important to pray, we need to understand *how* to pray.

Some Christians today will get in a prayer meeting, pray for four or five minutes, and then stop. They don't know what to do after a few minutes, so they get up and wander around the room, or they start reading their Bible, because they want to do something spiritual.

But when we've prayed to the best of our ability with our understanding, or in our native language, we have the Holy Spirit to help us pray. The Bible says, "Likewise the Spirit also helpeth our infirmities: for we know not what we should pray for as we ought: but the Spirit itself maketh intercession for us with groanings which cannot be uttered [in articulate speech]" (Rom. 8:26 *KJV*).

Let's look at the next verse in Romans chapter 8: "And he that searcheth the hearts knoweth what is the mind of the Spirit, because he maketh intercession for the saints according to the will of God" (v. 27 *KJV*).

We can say to the Lord, "I've prayed about this situation the best I know how to pray. Your Word says that the Holy Spirit would help me pray. So I'm going to pray in other tongues now, and I know that as I do, I will be praying according to Your perfect will."

'Praying Through'—a Forgotten Truth

Then when you start praying in other tongues, you're supposed to stay there and *pray*! Pentecostals used to call it "praying through." Many Charismatics today will say, "Well, we're not going to do that. We're just going to speak the Word and call it done by faith."

Certainly, when it comes to your own personal life, you can pray or "say" according to God's Word, and believe you receive your answer (Mark 11:23,24). Then that's it; you call it done by faith, and you rejoice and praise God until the answer is manifested. You are praising and thanking Him in advance because you believe you have received whatever it is you prayed for. And Jesus said you would *have* it (v. 24)!

However, very often, when it comes to other kinds of praying—praying for others, for example—you don't really know how to pray as you ought. You need to get hold of the heart of God on the matter, and get His power moving on behalf of that situation. You do that by praying in the Spirit and then staying with it until you're done or until you've "prayed through."

Now what do I mean by "prayed through"? It means you've prayed until you have a "release" or a note of victory on the inside, in your spirit.

Praying People Get Things Done!

In comparison to the old-time Pentecostals, many Christians today don't know much of anything about praying. I grew up witnessing powerful moves of God's Spirit and hearing testimony after testimony that came about as a result of people's praying and staying with it until they got the job done.

I want to be a part of bringing back that kind of diligence, determination, and fervency of spirit in prayer. I don't want to see us as believers having no power to change things because we are ignorant of this important Bible subject.

God Is No Respecter of Persons

Was there something special about those old-time Pentecostals who got answers when they prayed? Did God love them more than He loves us? The answer, of course, is no. The Bible says that the prayers of a righteous man (or woman) are powerful and effective (James 5:16). Well, are you a righteous one? If you have been born again, you are! And in that respect, the difference between us and those old-time Pentecostal "pray-ers" is, *nothing*!

2 CORINTHIANS 5:21 (KJV)

21 For he hath made him [Christ] **to be sin for us, who knew no sin; that we might BE MADE THE RIGHTEOUSNESS OF GOD IN HIM.**

Now let's look at James 5:16, which talks about what the prayers of the righteous can accomplish.

JAMES 5:16

16 Therefore confess your sins to each other and pray for each other so that you may be healed. THE PRAYER OF A RIGHTEOUS MAN IS POWERFUL AND EFFECTIVE.

What is "a righteous man," or a righteous person, according to this verse? Let's look at verses 17 and 18 at how the Bible describes one righteous man, the prophet Elijah.

JAMES 5:17,18

17 **Elijah was a man just like us. He prayed earnestly that it would not rain, and it did not rain on the land for three and a half years.**

18 **Again he prayed, and the heavens gave rain, and the earth produced its crops.**

The *King James Version* reads, "Elias [Elijah] was a man subject to like passions as we are . . ." (v. 17). In other words, Elijah was no different from you and me. Certainly, he was anointed by God, but Elijah had faults and shortcomings just like anyone else, and missed it at times just like we do. Yet James uses Elijah to illustrate a righteous man. Writing under the inspiration of the Holy Spirit, James said, ". . . The prayer of a righteous man is powerful and effective" (James 5:16). Then immediately after that, James said, "Elijah . . ." (v. 17).

This was the same Elijah who did exploits by the Spirit of God. He once called down fire from Heaven and slew 450 prophets of Baal. Then when Jezebel threatened him, Elijah ran away in fear for his life! Yet James still called him a righteous man.

A Body of 'Pray-ers'

Some people think that God will hear and answer the prayers of others, but won't hear their prayers. They might not feel important or worthy enough to have their prayers answered. But we just saw that the prayer of a righteous man or woman is powerful and effective! We also determined that if we are in Christ—if we've been born again—*we* are righteous! And we also saw that a righteous man or woman doesn't have to be perfect and never make any mistakes in order to pray effectively (James 5:17,18).

Where does that leave us? It leaves us in a position to pray! And not just to pray, but to pray effectively and powerfully! Acts 10:34 says, ". . . God is no respecter of persons" (*KJV*). That means God won't show favoritism to one righteous man or woman over another. He wants *every one of us* to pray!

Prayer and the Glory

In previous chapters, we saw in Second Chronicles chapter 5 that consecrating yourself, walking in love and unity, and giving thanks and praise to God were connected with experiencing the glory of God. Now let's look at chapter 7 to see the connection between *prayer* and the glory.

2 CHRONICLES 7:1-3

1 **When Solomon finished PRAYING, fire came down from heaven and consumed the burnt offering and the sacrifices, and THE GLORY OF THE LORD FILLED THE TEMPLE.**

2 **The priests could not enter the temple of the Lord because the glory of the Lord filled it.**

3 **When all the Israelites saw the fire coming down and the glory of the Lord above the temple, they knelt on**

the pavement with their faces to the ground, and they worshiped and gave thanks to the Lord, saying, "He is good; his love endures forever."

Notice that after Solomon prayed, the glory of God filled the temple. How does that apply to us today? Remember I said that, today, *we* are God's temple, the house in which He dwells. I believe that as we, the Church of the Lord Jesus Christ, give ourselves to praying and seeking God, the glory of God will fill the temple, the *Church*, individually and collectively. That means the glory of God will fill *us!*

Yes, supernatural manifestations of God's power can be wrought through prayer, as we saw in James 5:16, which says, ". . . The prayer of a righteous man is powerful and effective." In *The Amplified Bible*, that verse reads, ". . . The earnest (heartfelt, continued) prayer of a righteous man makes tremendous power available [dynamic in its working]"!

The Nine Gifts of the Holy Spirit

I believe we are going to witness more and more of the tremendous power of God that is dynamic in its working! In this book, we've read about some of the tremendous manifestations of the Spirit throughout the ages that many have witnessed or heard or read about. Now let's look at First Corinthians 12:7–11, which lists the nine gifts of the Spirit—gifts or manifestations that we should see occurring more and more as we enter into the greater glory.

1 CORINTHIANS 12:7–11 (KJV)

7 But the manifestation of the Spirit is given to every man
to profit withal.

8 For to one is given by the Spirit the WORD OF WISDOM;
to another the WORD OF KNOWLEDGE by the same
Spirit;

9 To another [the gift of special] FAITH by the same Spirit; to
another the GIFTS OF HEALING [or healings] by the same
Spirit;

10 To another the WORKING OF MIRACLES; to another
PROPHECY; to another DISCERNING OF SPIRITS; to
another DIVERS KINDS OF TONGUES; to another the
INTERPRETATION OF TONGUES:

11 But all these worketh that one and the selfsame Spirit,
dividing to every man severally as he will.

Often when we hear teaching about these gifts, we hear
them divided into three groups: (1) the *revelation* gifts,
which include the word of wisdom, the word of knowledge,
and discerning of spirits (vv. 8,10); (2) the *power* gifts, which
include the gift of faith, gifts of healings, and the working
of miracles (vv. 9,10); and (3) the *vocal* gifts, which include
prophecy, tongues, and interpretation of tongues (v. 10). We
should be hungering to see more of these gifts in manifestation in the Body of Christ, and I believe the way to satisfy
that hunger is through our praying to see more of these
manifestations.

At our church, we have been praying for some time for
greater and greater manifestations of the power of God. Lately,
we have particularly been praying for greater manifestations
of the power gifts: the gift of faith, gifts of healings, and the

working of miracles. These gifts were in manifestation in the Book of Acts, and we've heard of instances of their being in manifestation in modern history. I have been privileged to be used in the gifts of healings in many of my crusades. But we've not seen these gifts in our generation as God desires. In fact, the manifestations of the past are only a smattering compared to what God wants to do in these last days!

A Firsthand Experience

Lynette and I have a personal testimony concerning the manifestation of the gift of faith on behalf of a family member. Now when I talk about the gift of faith as listed in First Corinthians 12:9, I'm not talking about *general* faith or the faith that we all have and can develop to receive our needs met according to the promises in God's Word.

When I talk about the gift of faith, I'm talking about a supernatural operation or manifestation of the Spirit of God that secures the answer, even if for another, by a command of faith that will not be denied, regardless of the level to which an individual's general faith is developed. Although the manifestation of the answer may not occur instantaneously, that command of faith is as the voice of God, pronouncing it as done—and it will always come to pass.

Years ago, Lynette's aunt developed several life-threatening diseases, and her health greatly deteriorated. She had liver cancer, diabetes, and a heart condition. It seemed as if everything under the sun had gone wrong with her health!

She was finally put in a nursing home. The doctor gave her just a few weeks to live as the cancer had spread throughout her body.

Spiritually speaking, we had done all we knew to do for Lynette's aunt at the time. We prayed, asking God for her healing, but things seemed only to get worse. Lying there in that nursing home, her body was drawn up and feeble, and most of the time, she was curled up in her bed in a fetal position.

One Saturday morning as Lynette and I were getting dressed to go out, I heard Lynette shout from another room: "Aunt _____ will live and not die!"

The gift of faith had dropped into Lynette's heart. We didn't tell anyone about what happened, but a few days later, Lynette called her mother, asking about her aunt's condition.

"Hon, you wouldn't believe it," she said, "but she's getting better!"

And in a matter of about four weeks' time, Lynette's aunt was completely well and released from that nursing home! She was pronounced healed of liver cancer, diabetes (which she'd had for years), and the heart disease. She was up, walking around as if she'd never even been sick! And Lynette's aunt lived in complete health for many years afterward before she finally went home to be with the Lord.

What cured my wife's aunt? Was it her faith? Was it the faith of those of us around her who loved her and wanted to see her well? No, it was a supernatural manifestation of the gift of faith!

I think it's important to note here that the gifts of the Spirit, including the gift of special faith, manifest only as the Spirit wills, not as we will (1 Cor. 12:11). If we could cause the gifts to be manifested as *we* willed, we'd do it all the time, wouldn't we?

That is why we need to pray and seek God concerning the manifestation of these gifts. We need to see the power of God in demonstration in our generation.

I have lived long enough to see some of the outstanding miracles that took place during the Healing Revival of the '40s and '50s. But we're not seeing the moving of the Spirit of God today that we saw back then.

That can change! People need to know that God is still God and that He is still moving in the lives of people today. Certainly, some Christians in our day have experienced some of the same kinds of healings and miracles that others have only read about or heard someone else talk about. But these instances are relatively isolated and few and far between compared with the miracles of the past.

We need more than isolated instances of miracles here and there. We need to have these kinds of things happening continually—throughout the Body of Christ and throughout the world!

The Gifts of the Spirit Are All-Inclusive

Who can benefit from the working of the gifts of the Spirit? First Corinthians 12:7 tells us: "But the manifestation of the Spirit is given to every man to profit withal" (*KJV*). The *New International Version* says, *"Now to each one the manifestation of the Spirit is given for the common good."* Notice it says, *"Each one is given the manifestation of the Spirit."*

I want you to understand that the gifts of the Spirit were not designed to work only through those in a pulpit ministry. They were designed for the entire Body of Christ. God wants the entire Church, not just a few, to have the manifestation of the gifts of the Spirit in their lives.

Many Church members have the mistaken idea that if they're not called to a pulpit ministry, they won't have the gifts of the Spirit operating in their life. But that is simply not true. The last part of that verse says that to *each one* is given the manifestation ". . . for the common good." What does it mean, "for the common good"? It means that everyone in the group should benefit, and in this case, it's talking about the Body of Christ.

Let's look at verse 11 of First Corinthians 12: "But all these worketh that one and the selfsame Spirit, dividing to every man severally as he will" (*KJV*). In the *New International Version*, it reads, *"All these are the work of one and the same Spirit, and he gives them to each one, just as he determines."*

I have actually heard people say, "I have the gift of prophecy" or some other gift of the Spirit. But, no, they may be privileged to have that gift working in their lives at times, but they don't have, or own, that gift! It is a gift of the Holy Spirit, meaning it belongs to *Him*. He may use you in one or more of His gifts, but He does it as *He* wills or determines (1 Cor. 12:11), not as *you* will. In other words, you can't just turn the gifts of the Spirit on and off as you please.

Yet we may desire and seek after the gifts of the Spirit—we may pray—that they be manifested in our midst, because the Bible tells us to ". . . covet earnestly the best gifts . . ." (1 Cor. 12:31 *KJV*). The *New International Version* tells us to *"eagerly desire them."*

"Well, what are the best gifts?" someone asked.

The best gifts are the ones we need at the moment! Whether it be the word of wisdom, the word of knowledge, the gift of faith, the gifts of healings, the working of miracles, prophecy, discerning of spirits, tongues, or interpretation of tongues, the best gift to have in operation at any given time is the one you need!

I want to do my part in prayer concerning God's greater glory, and I believe you do too. God is inviting every one of us to take part in praying for the move of His Spirit in these last days. Those of us who are called by His Name have been made the righteousness of God through Jesus Christ (2 Cor. 5:21). And as "righteous ones," our praying can make tremendous power available, dynamic in its working, and enable us to see the results of our praying—the greater glory in our midst!

Chapter 15

THE GLORY OF GOD
Blessings for the Reverent

We need to understand the importance of reverencing and respecting the moving of the Spirit, and of learning to properly cooperate with and yield to what He is doing in our midst. If we don't reverence the things of God, we will grieve the Spirit of God and miss experiencing the move of the Spirit that He wants us to experience.

My own observations of people grieving the Holy Spirit when He is moving in a service or meeting is that they don't do it intentionally, but, rather, ignorantly. They have not been taught regarding how to respond to a move of the Spirit. In this chapter, we're going to talk about key number nine to experiencing the glory, and that is *reverence.*

Key Number Nine: *Reverence*

As many might know, I grew up in a Pentecostal denomination, and I am very familiar with the moving of the Spirit of God. I want to share with you some of my observations concerning reverence toward the things of the Spirit then and now. I believe they will help us in our cooperation with God as He begins to manifest His greater glory in the earth.

Growing up, and even as a young man, I noticed that one thing you never saw when the Spirit of God was moving in a service was people clapping or shouting, especially if someone was prophesying or giving out a message in tongues or interpretation of tongues. Everyone, including the young people, was silent before God. When someone in a service was speaking by the unction of the Holy Spirit, people bowed their heads in reverence and in awe of the power and Presence of God. They closed their eyes and listened reverently to what the Lord was saying.

I see that today too. But very often, I also see people begin to clap or shout before someone is done giving out a message by the unction of the Spirit, and others in the congregation can't even hear what is being said. That grieves the Holy Spirit, and He will not continue to move in an atmosphere where He is not reverenced.

Irreverence Will Rob Us of the Full Blessing and Manifestation of God's Power

So many times today, if someone begins to prophesy, people will clap and shout, "Hallelujah!" or "Glory!" and others can't even hear what the Spirit of God is saying. The people miss out on the blessing God intends because some are acting irreverent. I didn't say they *mean* to be irreverent and disrespectful of the things of God. As I said, they are largely untaught and don't understand that we must have an attitude of reverence toward the things of God.

The reason the Holy Spirit begins to move in a service and then the power seems to suddenly wane is because people demonstrate so loudly that the Spirit is grieved, and then He stops moving. He can't accomplish what He wants to accomplish because the people don't know how to act.

Certainly, there is a time to shout in church and give praise and glory to God with a loud voice. It's not good or right never to display joy and enthusiasm in church. Ecclesiastes 3:1 says, *"There is a time for everything, and a season for every activity under heaven."* There is a time to clap, shout, dance, and run. But we should know when it's time to be quiet and when it's time to shout! We should learn the difference. We will grieve the Spirit of God if we don't.

Now, I'm not talking about having a solemn attitude all the time and calling that reverence. Christians who are like that don't have any joy. They're missing out on the joy of their salvation. No, I'm talking about showing a true reverence for God in which people respect and yield to what He is doing at any given time.

Bible Understanding Will Help Us Reverence the Moving of the Spirit

I think the problem is that some people don't understand the moving of the Spirit. They sense the anointing in a service during the altar call, for example, in which the unsaved are being invited to receive Jesus as Savior. But instead of yielding to that anointing and praying in the Spirit for the lost who are present, they jump up and try to prophesy or give out some message from the Lord. And it interrupts what the Holy Spirit is trying to do at that moment in the service. Very often, it may cost someone an opportunity to become born again.

Someone might say, "Well, the Spirit was moving, wasn't He?"

Yes, but the Holy Spirit does not interrupt Himself! He does things decently and in order, because the Bible says that God is not a God of confusion, but of peace (1 Cor. 14:33).

Not only that, the preceding verse, First Corinthians 14:32, says, *"The spirits of prophets are subject to the control of prophets."*

In other words, when someone is prophesying or speaking in other tongues, he or she is in control of his or her speaking. That person can yield or not yield, and start or stop speaking whenever he or she wants to.

The Holy Spirit doesn't take anyone over. He's a Gentleman, so to speak. He prompts you, and you yield to Him. *You* have control of your own voice.

Many years ago when I was in a tent meeting in Michigan, there was a woman on the front row who caused such a commotion that she had to be escorted out of the service. The ushers tried to get her to quiet down because she was interrupting the service. But she refused, and when they tried to lead her out of the service, she tensed up, became as stiff as a board, and had to be carried out!

The entire time, she insisted, "But I can't help it! When the Spirit gets to moving, I *have* to do this!" One minister who was trying to help this woman said, "No, you *don't* have to do this. That is not scriptural. The Bible says that the spirit of the prophets is subject to the prophets. If there is a power taking you over and controlling you, it's not God's power."

But the woman wouldn't listen. The ushers told her, "You're free to go back in to the service if you won't interrupt anymore."

She replied, "I can't promise that, because if the power moves on me, I have to do it!"

I've actually heard people scream and yell so loudly during a move of the Holy Spirit that it made people sort of jump because they were so startled. I'm talking about "blood-curdling" screams! We should know that it is not the Spirit of God making them do that.

It is irreverent to make noise and cause commotion when a minister is ministering or when he or someone else is prophesying or giving out a word from the Lord. When people scream, it pulls people out of the glory, so to speak, and back into the natural, and it becomes more difficult for them to get back into the Spirit so they can pay attention to what the Lord is doing. And they can miss some important things that God wanted them to hear.

As I said, there is a time when it is appropriate to shout unto God and to rejoice in His Presence. But there is also a time to be silent before Him, in reverent awe.

There Is a Purpose for
Every Move of God's Spirit

There's nothing wrong with being joyful before the Lord or even clapping your hands to the beat of the music. Many people misunderstood my dad when he taught the message years ago called, "Plans, Purposes, and Pursuits." He even wrote a book by the same title, and some people still didn't get it. They said that he was against clapping your hands in a service.

But that's not what he said at all. It's all right to clap your hands at certain times, such as in time with the music. But Dad was talking about there being a right time to clap and a wrong time to clap. For example, it is wrong to clap, holler, and shout when the Spirit of God is moving and ministering to people, such as when a minister is prophesying to individuals or to a crowd. Clapping and making a lot of noise while the minister is speaking by the inspiration of the Holy Spirit grieves the Spirit and dissipates the power of God. Dad was simply talking about reverencing the move of the Spirit of God.

Treating the Things of God as Common
Can Hinder His Moving in Our Midst

To give you another example of our lack of reverence for spiritual things today, many pastors don't regularly hold Communion services in their churches. Some pastors just sort of tack on the distributing of the Communion elements at the end of a service without ever teaching on what those elements, the juice and the wafer, symbolize: the blood and the broken body of our Lord. Others rarely hold any kind of Communion service at all.

Someone once asked me, "How can you hold a Communion service for a church your size every first Sunday of the month?"

I answered, "We just do it—because Communion is an ordinance of the Church" (1 Cor. 11:24–26)!

Communion is the essence of the Gospel summed up in two emblems, and we know that these emblems symbolize the blood and the broken body of Jesus Christ. What a vast number of sermons you could preach on the blood that was shed and the body that was broken for the sins of mankind!

The Name and the Glory

Sometimes I don't think we honor the Name of Jesus as we should. It seems that many of us don't hold in remembrance Jesus' great act of love for God and for mankind with His death on the Cross. One way we can show reverence for God and for the move of His Spirit is to honor His Son, who bore our sin and shame in dying on that cross.

Remember, from the time of man's creation, God's original intention was that man have unbroken fellowship with Himself. When Adam sinned, his sin separated him from a holy God. But the Cross of Christ became a bridge whereby mankind could once again enjoy fellowship with the Father.

Through the precious Name of Jesus, we can freely, with confidence, enter His Presence. Because of what Jesus did through His death, burial, and resurrection, mankind can be in holy union with God Almighty!

Think about that! Jesus has been given the Name that is above every name. That Name has delivered us from the power of darkness and has brought us into the Kingdom of God. And we have that Name today to set us free from whatever bondage the enemy tries to bring our way.

I received a special revelation of that Name when I was a youth minister in the 1960s. We had invited André Crouch, who was just getting started in the ministry, to help us hold a youth rally in Dallas. He accepted, and we filled a high-school auditorium to overflowing with young people who came to hear him minister.

As he began ministering, he gave a testimony about a time he had been invited to be a guest performer at a rock concert. He related that the music was wild, and that by the time it was his turn to take the stage, the crowd was pretty rowdy. He asked the Lord, *What am I going to do?*

He took his seat at a piano amidst a roar of screaming voices and began softly playing arpeggios up and down those keys. Then he began saying the Name, "Jesus." He had only spoken that wonderful Name three times when you could have heard a pin drop amid the 10,000 people who were present at that rock concert. All eyes became riveted to the platform.

André then began to play and sing. Afterward, he told the crowd, "If you want to know more about the power you just sensed here, meet me backstage and I'll tell you more." Hundreds of people met him that day—all because of the awesome power in the Name of Jesus.

We need never be afraid when we understand what that Name represents. The devil is afraid of that Name, and rightly so. Jesus whipped him and took away the keys of death and hell and arose victorious over him (*see* Revelation 1:18). Jesus conquered death so that all who accept Him as Savior and call upon His Name shall be saved from eternal death and shall gain eternal life (John 3:16; Rom. 10:13).

That is why Paul could say, "O death, where is thy sting? O grave, where is thy victory?" (1 Cor. 15:55 *KJV*). Because of Jesus, we don't have to die. Certainly, if Jesus tarries His coming, our physical body will die one day. But as Christians, when we leave our earthly body, we will be with Jesus! We will remain alive with Him forevermore!

As I said, to reverence God doesn't mean we are solemn and sad. It doesn't mean we can't have any joy or be happy in life. But it does mean that when the Spirit of God is working in our midst, we should respect Him and yield to what He wants to do, not to what we want to do or to the way we think the service or meeting should go. As we learn to flow with the Spirit of God and practice reverencing Him in our midst, I believe we will experience greater and greater blessings of the manifest glory of God.

Chapter 16

THE SIGNIFICANCE OF THE GLORY

We have seen that throughout history, God has been faithful to manifest His glory on behalf of His people. And we have seen in the Bible that at times, God's glory was manifested as a cloud. At other times, the glory was referred to as a bright light. But consistently, we observe that when the glory of God was in manifestation, it was always a time of revelation and change.

Changed by God's Glory

Let's look at how the glory of God can change the believer so that he or she can be used to manifest greater measures of the glory to others.

2 CORINTHIANS 3:13,17,18 (KJV)

13 And not as Moses, which put a vail over his face, that the children of Israel could not stedfastly look to the end of that which is abolished:

17 Now the Lord is that Spirit: and where the Spirit of the Lord is, there is liberty.

18 But we all, with open face beholding as in a glass the glory of the Lord, are CHANGED into the same image from glory to glory, even as by the Spirit of the Lord.

I want you to notice it says we are ". . . CHANGED into the same image FROM GLORY TO GLORY . . . ." The phrase, "changed from glory to glory," implies that there is an ever-present action taking place. It didn't say, "You *have been* changed." If it had, that would have meant it has already taken place; it would be all over, and in terms of our walking in His likeness, where we're at today would be as good as it gets!

The *New International Version* says we are, ". . . being *transformed into his likeness with ever-increasing glory . . . .*"

So, according to Second Corinthians 3:18, as we behold the glory of the Lord, we will be changed from glory to glory, or with ever-increasing glory, into His likeness. That means the more we get to know the Lord as we walk with Him, the more we will become transformed, or changed, with His ever-increasing glory. And as we are transformed with ever-increasing glory into His likeness, it will affect every area of our lives.

Now look at the phrase in Second Corinthians 3:18, ". . . with OPEN FACE beholding . . . ." The *New International Version* says, ". . . *with unveiled faces . . . .*" In Exodus 34, we read that when Moses climbed Mount Sinai to receive the Ten Commandments, the glory of God shone so brightly upon Moses' face that he had to wear a veil when he came back down among the people (vv. 33–35). But Second Corinthians 3:18 says that we can behold God's glory with "unveiled faces"! In other words, nothing should obscure our view of God's glory.

To give you a natural illustration of God's glory being obscured from our view, have you ever tried to look in a bathroom mirror after someone just finished taking a shower? The mirror is usually "fogged" or steamed up, and you can't see very much in the mirror until you wipe it off.

So how do we get more of the glory of God in our lives? How do we behold His glory "with unveiled faces" and change "with ever-increasing glory" into His likeness? In a manner of speaking, we need to wipe the fog off the mirror! We need to get rid of anything in our lives that would hinder our view of Him and our reflection of Him.

In Chapters 9 through 15, I discussed nine keys that I believe we in the Body of Christ can practice to experience a greater measure of the glory of God. In review, those nine keys are as follows:

1. **Obedience**
2. **Drawing near to God**
3. **Consecration**
4. **Walking in unity before God**
5. **Giving thanks to God**
6. **Giving praise to God**
7. **Worshipping God**

8. Prayer

9. Reverence

We need to use these nine keys to experience more of the glory of God in our lives. Practicing these things will keep us from fogging up our mirror, so to speak. We need to continually ask ourselves, "Is disobedience in some area of my life standing in my way of reflecting God's glory?" "Am I drawing near to God as I should?" "Am I lacking in consecration to Him?" "Am I walking in love and unity with my fellow man as I should?" "Am I overflowing with thanks, praise, and worship to God?" "Am I honoring God in my prayer life and in my reverence of Him?"

I'm not telling you to ask these questions so that you can go digging for all your failures and shortcomings and use them to heap condemnation upon yourself. We simply need to ask the questions so that we are continually drawing near to God and beholding His glory. Then we can be changed and receive greater and greater measures of His glory in our lives.

The Bible says that when Jesus comes back for His Church, *all of us* who are born again will be changed. *"In the twinkling of an eye,"* we will be changed and caught up to meet Him in the air (*see* 1 Thess. 4:16,17).

1 CORINTHIANS 15:51,52

51 Listen, I tell you a mystery: We will not all sleep, but WE WILL ALL BE CHANGED—

52 in a flash, in the twinkling of an eye, at the last trumpet. For the trumpet will sound, the dead will be raised imperishable, and WE WILL BE CHANGED.

These verses are talking about what we call the Rapture or the "catching away" of the Church, in which mortality will put on immortality, and corruptible flesh will be changed into that which is incorruptible or imperishable. It will be a glorious day when that trump sounds and we are caught up to meet our Lord and Savior!

But we don't have to wait until that time to be changed by God's glory. I'm not talking about being changed from mortal to immortal as in the "catching away"; I'm talking about coming under the influence of the Presence and power of God until we are changed from faith to faith, glory to glory, and strength to strength.

If we are born again—indwelt by the glory and Presence of God—we as mortal beings can be changed *in this life* as we behold His glory and allow ourselves to be changed. And as we are changed "from glory to glory," we can be used as vessels to manifest God's glory in the earth.

But whether or not we experience and partake of God's greater glory here on the earth will be up to us, not God. The glory has been made available; God has made His will known concerning His glory on the earth. But whether or not we will tap into that power and glory is for us to decide.

The Glory Is Not Just for Ourselves, but for *Others!*

We are living in times in which we desperately need to experience the ever-increasing glory of God. All we have to do is look around at everything the enemy is trying to do to know that we are living in the last days. The devil knows his time is short, and he is increasing his activity upon the earth. As never before, we need to display the ever-increasing glory of God to the world.

Most of us have heard testimonies of spectacular manifestations of God's glory in various countries around the world. God manifests His glory to set people free, because Christians in those countries dare to hold forth the Word of truth in places where the manifestation of the enemy is rampant.

Some of these places are charged with the presence of devils and demons. Witch doctors and spiritists engage people in devil worship and cult practices. As a result, they fall into cruel bondage and oppression. In fact, in some places, many are demon-possessed.

Some in those countries have witnessed chairs and other objects floating across a room by the operation of demon power. In our country, people usually see those kinds of things only in movies. But it is a reality in other places in the world.

Even in America, cult practices are on the rise, and they have found their way into every avenue of our media and communications. For example, people get on television and claim to be able to see into people's lives and tell them things, similar to the way the Holy Ghost might manifest Himself in a word of knowledge. But these "fortune-tellers" are counterfeits of the real thing: the power and glory of God Almighty!

Others claim the ability to have conversations with loved ones who have passed away. But if there is any accuracy to what they see and hear, it is coming from another power, not the power of God. Those men and women are operating by familiar spirits—demon spirits—that tell them certain things about people's lives, and, sadly, it leads many astray.

The Holy Spirit knows everything, and He can reveal truth to the hearts of men and women that can change their lives for the better. And He is greater (1 John 4:4)! The Greater One can put to naught the bondage and havoc wrought in people's lives by the enemy. But it's going to take Christians knowing how to yield to and flow with Him.

Do you want more of the glory? It's in the midst of the glory that God can do His perfect work in our lives if we yield to Him. We need to allow ourselves to be changed by the power and glory of God so that we can become vessels that will manifest His glory to the world.

The Glory of God Can Bring Revelation

The glory of God brings change, but it can also bring revelation. In the glory and Presence of God, we can see things that we wouldn't otherwise see. For example, God led Moses to climb a mountain, where God revealed to him the Promised Land (Deut. 34:1–3).

Now, spiritually speaking, "going up to the mountain" could be compared to being in the manifest Presence and glory of God. And isn't it in those times that God shows us our "promised land"—the things He wants us to possess in our lives and ministries? He gives us glimpses of our future so that we can do something about it—so we can get into that divine flow and cooperate with Him in faith so He can bring it all to pass.

Did you know that you can't do something about what you don't know about? That's why God gives you a vision, or a dream, in your heart about your future. And that's how you're able to advance and go on and do what God has shown you to do, even in the midst of difficulties and trials.

Have you ever heard of people talk about having a "mountaintop experience"? They're talking about having a time of intimacy with the Lord in His Presence, where the things of the world and the cares of life become dim and insignificant in comparison with His glory.

I think we can come to a place where we are living more and more on the mountaintop—in a greater glory. I'm not talking about being "so heavenly minded that we're no earthly good." I'm talking about living in the Presence of God in such a way that we can be changed more into His likeness, so that we can positively affect the lives of those around us with what we have of Him.

I want to look briefly into the life of an Old Testament prophet, the prophet Isaiah, who saw his own need for change when he encountered the glory of God. Isaiah 6:1–8 outlines this supernatural encounter and the effect it wrought in Isaiah's life.

ISAIAH 6:1–8

1 In the year that King Uzziah died, I saw the Lord seated on a throne, high and exalted, and the train of his robe filled the temple.

2 Above him were seraphs, each with six wings: With two wings they covered their faces, with two they covered their feet, and with two they were flying.

3 And they were calling to one another: "Holy, holy, holy is the Lord Almighty; the whole earth is full of his glory."

4 At the sound of their voices the doorposts and thresholds shook and the temple was filled with smoke.

5 "Woe to me!" I cried. "I am ruined! For I am a man of unclean lips, and I live among a people of unclean lips, and my eyes have seen the King, the Lord Almighty."

6 Then one of the seraphs flew to me with a live coal in his hand, which he had taken with tongs from the altar.

7 With it he touched my mouth and said, "See, this has touched your lips; your guilt is taken away and your sin atoned for."

8 Then I heard the voice of the Lord saying, "Whom shall I send? And who will go for us?" And I said, "Here am I. Send me!"

Isaiah was an Israelite, a man in covenant with God. Yet in the midst of the glory of God, he saw how unfit for service he really was. He saw his need for change. He said, " *'Woe to me! . . . . I am ruined! For I am a man of unclean lips, and I live among a people of unclean lips, and my eyes have seen the King, the Lord Almighty"* (v. 5).

When Isaiah cried out, one of the angels took a burning coal from the altar and, with it, touched Isaiah's lips, saying, " *. . . 'See, this has touched your lips; your guilt is taken away and your sin atoned for' "* (v. 7). Isaiah became a changed man.

— 219 —

In the midst of a manifestation of the glory of God, Isaiah became someone God could use. Do *you* want to be someone God can use? If you do, get in the Presence of Almighty God and let Him change you.

There are changes we all need to make. But sometimes, we can't even see some of the things we need to change until we get in the light of the glory of God, where He can show us those things.

To illustrate this in the natural, if you were to build a racing engine for an automobile, you might inspect the heads on that engine, and, to the naked eye, they might look fine. But you can send them to a special place where they use what is called a magnifying flux to get a better picture of the condition of that engine. A magnifying flux is a special kind of lighted magnifier that enables mechanics and technicians to see even small cracks in the engine that are undetectable to the naked eye. If that engine is going to function optimally, it needs to be checked under a magnifying flux.

Similarly, we need to get under the "magnifying flux" of the glory of God! And in the light of *His* light, we will be able to see the flaws and areas of our lives that we need to change so that we can partake of more of Him. We'll have a greater capacity for His glory when we've gotten rid of those things that hinder us in our spiritual walk. Then we can press on toward our future goal or prize and finish our course with joy!

Do you know why some people are never changed by the glory? It could be because they haven't allowed God's power into their lives to change them. Maybe it has been through ignorance; perhaps they haven't even realized or understood that such power exists. They are ignorant of the mighty power of the Holy Spirit in the life of the believer.

Others are acquainted with the working of the power of God in the life of the believer, but they've never allowed the power of God to *finish* its work in their lives.

There will always be those who never enter into the fullness of God and His glory. Some will remain willfully ignorant. Maybe they are too interested in the things of the world to have a place in their lives for the things of God. I don't know all the reasons why people choose not to accept the fullness of God's Spirit, but I won't be one of those people!

God can do so much for and through us when we are yielded to Him and hunger for manifestations of His glory. When the glory of God is in manifestation, it is easier to receive from Him, because you are more conscious of Him than of natural things. You're more yielded to the things of the Spirit than to the things of the natural world around you. Your resistance to spiritual things is at low tide, so to speak. Your mind is not busy with the crashing waves of the cares and the trials of life; you are focusing on Him.

As you are completely focused on God and His Word— *"beholding as in a glass, or mirror, the glory of the Lord"*— you are ready to act on His Word and do what He tells you to do. You become a willing vessel who can manifest His glory to the world around you.

Do you want to be changed by the glory of God? Then draw near to Him. Seek His face and then yield to Him as He begins to change you. He will lead you in the way that you should go, and you will glorify Him for the great things that He will do through you!

Chapter 17

TIMES OF REFRESHING IN THE PRESENCE OF THE LORD

In previous chapters, we talked about various ways that the Holy Spirit moves in our midst to bless, heal, and deliver those who will yield to and respect His Presence. One type of manifestation of God's Presence that we have not touched on is that concerning His refreshing. God desires to provide times of refreshing for His people, giving them the "fresh oil" of His Spirit to revive and strengthen them in their time of need.

ACTS 3:19 (KJV)

19 Repent ye therefore, and be converted, that your sins may be blotted out, when the TIMES OF REFRESHING SHALL COME FROM THE PRESENCE OF THE LORD.

Figuratively, "times of refreshing" in this verse refers to revival. What is revival? Simply put, it refers to a *reviving* of something. Now, that is not a bad thing. In times past, some in Charismatic circles thought you were being negative if you said we needed revival. But no, we all need to be revived or refreshed from time to time.

To be "revived" simply means, *to be brought back to a healthy, vigorous, or flourishing condition after a decline.* Literally, it is *recovering your breath*!

Have you ever watched a football game in which a player runs long with the ball—say, 80 or 90 yards—and then the next thing you see is the guy over on the sidelines breathing from an oxygen mask? What was he doing? He was refreshing himself. He was recovering his breath!

I used to run track, and I remember that as I finished running a race, I sometimes could hardly breathe. Now some people will just stand there and pant and breathe heavily after exerting themselves like that. But doing that isn't good for you, and it doesn't recover your breath.

When you finish a race, you should walk around for a while, drawing long breaths and letting them out slowly. That is the proper way to recover your breath. When you pant, you only fill the top of your lungs with oxygen. But when you take long breaths, you are filling your lungs to capacity, and that is how your body makes its recovery.

Spiritually speaking, that's why we need to get into the Presence of God and spend time taking long breaths of the Spirit—so that we can recover ourselves spiritually. When we do that, we are gaining strength and vitality in the Presence of God. The Presence of God is where we become saturated with God's strength and energy so that we can go out and accomplish what we need to accomplish in life.

Spiritual 'R and R'

Just because you are a Christian and you love God, believe His Word, and quote His Word doesn't mean that the pressures of life won't tax and strain you mentally, emotionally, and even physically at times. Some of us are so busy on our jobs that we need to take time in God's Presence just to quiet our mind and recover our breath, spiritually speaking. We need some spiritual "R & R," or some spiritual rest and relaxation!

Some people have so much going on with jobs, kids, and other responsibilities that they often don't take the time they need at home to recover themselves. They go to church to catch their breath. They've been on "go" for days on end, and they go to church to soak in the anointing and recover their strength.

People go to church to catch their breath, not to be beaten down by the minister telling them, "do this," or "don't do that." When the pressures of life seem overwhelming, people need to go to church to be refreshed. But when all they hear from the pulpit is preaching on "dos" and "don'ts," they'll run *from* church . . . not *to* church in their time of need.

Times of Refreshing Can Affect Your Sight

Have you ever been so weary in your mind that the future looked dim, uncertain, or even hopeless? When we get into the Presence of God, we can see new possibilities. Our vision becomes affected in the Presence of God. We see things differently! Our ability to see the future is enhanced. We become aware of what can happen with God. It's no longer the same old routine, the same "six and seven."

The Spirit of God wants to bless you. He wants to help you. He wants to carry you through! The Spirit of God wants to minister to you and make His Presence known in your life. But you have to take the time to relax in His Presence and allow Him to do it. I'm not talking about physical rest, although we do need adequate sleep and rest to stay healthy. I'm talking about *spiritual* rest and recovery.

Sometimes we press too hard. By that, I mean we press hard in our own strength to accomplish our daily tasks and our responsibilities. Certainly, our worship of God includes our physical strength, because the Bible says we are to love the Lord our God with all of our spirit, soul, and body. But once we've read, studied, and meditated on the Word, we need to allow God to bring to pass in our lives what we are trusting Him to do. Zechariah 4:6 says, ". . . *'Not by might nor by power, but by my Spirit,' says the Lord Almighty."*

Times of Refreshing Can Affect Your Hearing

Sometimes Christians will try so hard to hear from God that they wear themselves out, and they end up frustrated because they're not hearing anything. But it's as we attend to His Word, fellowship with Him in prayer, and just rest in Him that we begin to hear what He is saying to us.

— 226 —

In the tests and trials of life, so many Christians will give it all they've got in their own strength and then just give up and quit when their strength runs out. They don't hold on to what they know, because they've been holding on in their own strength. But victory comes in the morning! Victory comes when God's Word becomes such a part of us that we allow that Word to hold on to *us* even when darkness seems to loom like a cloud. And the Word of God *will* hold us up and see us through if we will not forsake it—if we will not give up and quit.

Let's look at our text again.

ACTS 3:19 (KJV)

19 REPENT ye therefore, and BE CONVERTED, that your sins may be blotted out, when the times of refreshing shall come from the presence of the Lord.

Often we are not experiencing revival and refreshing in the Presence of the Lord because we've allowed things to stand between us and God's manifest Presence. It all goes back to putting ourselves in position to experience that which God has made available and that which He desires to do.

Repentance: A Requisite for Experiencing God's Refreshing

As I said, God wants to bless you. He wants to help you. The Spirit of God wants to minister to you, meet your needs, and use you as a vessel unto honor (2 Timothy 2:21) to manifest His glory in the earth. But just because He desires to

— 227 —

move in your life doesn't mean that it's just automatically going to happen. According to this verse, if needed, we must first repent in order to experience those times of refreshing when they come.

Now, I understand the context in which Acts 3:19 was written. Peter was testifying before unsaved men. You might say, "Well, I've already repented then; I've already been born again."

Yes, there is a repentance or turning when one is born again. But the New Birth is much more than that. Second Corinthians 5:17 says, *"Therefore, if anyone is in Christ, he is a new creation; the old has gone, the new has come!"* The *King James Version* says, "Therefore if any man be in Christ, he is a new creature: old things are passed away; behold, all things are become new."

In the New Birth, our spirits are made brand-new! God took our spirit and made it brand-new—a new creation—in Christ.

So, yes, there is a repentance in the New Birth. And when we become born again, there is a certain refreshing that comes to us, because we are experiencing God's Presence in a way we never have before.

But after we are saved, it is possible for us to miss it and sin. And there needs to be a repenting or a turning from that. When we are sorry for our sin and ask God to forgive us, thank God, He does forgive! In fact, the Bible says He is faithful and just to forgive our sins and to cleanse us from all unrighteousness (1 John 1:9). We must then turn from sin, or *repent*. In other words, we can't have a casual attitude toward sin.

"Yes, Reverend Hagin," someone might say, "but I'm not committing any *big* sin."

I'm not even talking about what some might call "big" sins, such as murder, adultery, and so forth. It might just be that someone is harboring a bad attitude, and that wrong attitude is keeping him or her from experiencing times of refreshing in God's Presence.

Many people look at repentance in a negative way. But it is actually a positive thing, and we need to look at it from a positive standpoint. Repenting or turning from things that don't line up with God's Word—from things that displease Him—puts us in position to receive the blessings and benefits of His Word. It puts us in position to walk closely with Him and to enjoy not only His fellowship but His favor, guidance, protection, and so forth.

This verse, Acts 3:19, indicates that first, repentance is necessary to receive from God in the times when God manifests Himself. If you're not saved, certainly your repentance would mean accepting Jesus Christ as Savior and becoming born again.

'Love Works No Ill'

If you *are* saved, your repentance might mean asking God to forgive you for something He's been dealing with you about, such as some wrong you committed against someone.

Maybe you gossipped about someone; you shared something about someone else that you should have kept to yourself, and you damaged his or her reputation in the process. Even if what you said was true, it still could hurt that person, and the Bible says that love works no ill, or hurt, to its neighbor (Rom. 13:10). Before you say something about someone else, you need to ask yourself, *How is what I'm saying about this person going to affect him or her?*

Unfortunately what usually happens, when someone misses it is that as soon as some people find out about it, they'll pick up the phone and call someone else. They'll say, "Have you heard about So-and-so?" Usually, they'll add something, such as, "I'm only sharing this because I want you to pray about it." And they proceed to spread gossip. If you happen to be the one hearing about it, their "garbage can" mouths will make your ears "garbage can" ears!

When someone says to me, "Have you heard such-and-such about So-and-so?" and proceeds to gossip about the person, I say, "I'm sorry, but I don't want to hear that."

Now, of course, as pastor of RHEMA Bible Church, I have to listen to members of my staff, for example, if they need to relate something to me about a member of our congregation, especially as it pertains to that person's welfare. As a pastor, I am concerned about the well-being of my church members. But that doesn't mean I have to allow my ears to be filled up with a bunch of negative remarks about people that don't amount to anything more than gossip!

My ears aren't garbage cans, and neither are yours! You do not have to listen to people tear down others with their words. Just listening to gossip, even if you don't say anything yourself, can still have a negative effect on you.

And did you know that most of what you hear about someone else isn't true, anyway? Usually, every time someone passes on gossip about someone else, something new gets added to the story. Eventually, the account of what happened isn't anywhere close to the real truth.

Have you ever played the group game in which everyone stood in two lines, and each person passed information down to the next to see which person at the end of the lines could repeat the information most accurately?

The person at the head of each line whispers a line or phrase to the person behind him or her. Then that person, in turn, repeats the phrase quietly to the person behind him or her. This goes on until the last person is reached in each of the lines. Then those two say out loud what they heard. Most of the time, what is said at the end of the line isn't anything close to what was said at the beginning!

"Yes, but what if what you're saying about someone is absolutely true?" someone might ask.

Yes, but has the person doing the gossiping ever read Philippians 4:8, which says, "Finally, brothers, whatever is true, whatever is noble, whatever is right, whatever is pure, whatever is lovely, whatever is admirable—if anything is excellent or praiseworthy—think about such things"?

What he or she is saying about that other person may be true, but is it pure? Is it lovely? So, you see, just because something is true doesn't give us license to talk about it.

I took some time to talk about gossiping because of the devastating effect it can have on people, even an entire congregation, if it isn't stopped. This is just one area in which we may need to repent.

Conversion After the New Birth

Acts 3:19 indicates that repentance is necessary to receive from God in the times when God manifests Himself. Second, it indicates that we must be *converted*.

To "convert" something means to *change* it.

To illustrate this in the natural, in most places in the United States, there are 220 volts of electricity coming into a building or room to provide light or power. But in wiring the building, electricians "convert" those 220 volts at the breaker box to 110 volts of power. They split those volts, changing them at the point of contact from 220 to 110 volts.

Now in other countries, those volts aren't split, or changed. That's why when you travel to those places, you have to use a converter, which changes the volts for you from 220 to 110. Otherwise, if you plugged in your appliance and turned it on, those 220 volts would ruin it.

When something is converted, it is changed. Again, Acts 3:19 is in context referring to being born again. However, there is still a change that needs to take place after experiencing salvation—but not in your re-created spirit.

We already read that *"If anyone is in Christ, he is a new creation; the old has gone, the new has come!"* (2 Cor. 5:17). When you became born again, your spirit was changed; in fact, it was made brand-new. So your born-again spirit doesn't need to be converted, or changed, again. God made it spotless in the New Birth. Just a few verses down from Second Corinthians 5:17, Paul wrote, *"God made him [Jesus] who had no sin to be sin for us, so that in him we might become the righteousness of God"* (2 Cor. 5:21)!

Renew Your Mind and Be Refreshed in God's Presence

Then what change needs to take place after you are born again and become a new creation in Christ? Your spirit is changed, but your mind is not. The change I'm talking about is the process of changing your thinking or *renewing your mind*.

ROMANS 12:2

2 **Do not conform any longer to the pattern of this world, but BE TRANSFORMED BY THE RENEWING OF YOUR MIND. Then you will be able to test and approve what God's will is—his good, pleasing and perfect will.**

Many people become born again, but they never convert their thinking; they never change their thinking to line up with God's Word. By failing to renew their mind to think as God thinks, they miss out on receiving many of the blessings

He has provided for them. And, very often, they slide right back into their old lifestyle. It's not that they weren't sincere about accepting Jesus Christ as Savior and becoming born again. They simply failed to convert their thinking afterward, and it caused them to fall back into living the way they lived before they were saved.

Here is a simple illustration to show you what I mean. Suppose you changed your residence from one country to another that uses a different currency, but you never converted your money. You would not be living up to the standard of that country without money to spend. You wouldn't even enjoy basic benefits, such as food, clothing, or most anything else. You're in the new country, all right, but you're going to have to convert your currency—you're going to have to convert to the way people conduct business in that country—if you're going to enjoy the benefits of living in that new country.

Now, this conversion I'm talking about is not instantaneous; it is a process. In the New Birth, your spirit becomes brand-new the instant you accept Jesus Christ as Savior. But renewing your mind—converting your thinking to God's way of thinking—is an ongoing process.

Thank God, His times of refreshing can be ongoing too! We don't just get refreshed once and for all in the New Birth, and that's it. No, in our time of need God desires that, we find rest, refreshing, and recovery in His Presence. As we continually walk closely with Him and renew our minds with

His Word, we will position ourselves to receive of His glory and find the refreshing we need in the Presence of the Lord.

Recognizing the Times

We looked at two requisites for experiencing times of refreshing in the Presence of the Lord. Acts 3:19 says, "REPENT ye therefore, and BE CONVERTED, that your sins may be blotted out, when the times of refreshing shall come from the presence of the Lord" (*KJV*).

There is a third requisite to experiencing the glory and Presence of God when He manifests Himself, and that is, *we must recognize the times.*

ECCLESIASTES 3:1 (KJV)

1 To every thing there is a season, and a time to every purpose under the heaven.

In this verse, notice how *times* and *purposes* are connected. God manifests Himself to accomplish His purpose in the lives of people on earth. And this verse says that there is a season, or time, for every purpose under Heaven.

Just as a side thought, I think what has happened with many Christians who have turned their backs on the faith message is that somehow they expected to plant a crop and then reap a harvest the next day. They didn't recognize that there is seedtime, or planting time, and then there's harvest time. Reaping the rewards of your faith doesn't often happen overnight.

Just in the natural, if you're planting a crop—let's say, cotton, for example—you have to make sure the ground is tilled properly and is ready for planting—ready to receive the seed.

Then once the crop begins to grow and emerge from the soil, you have to make sure the boll weevils don't take over the crop. You have to make sure the weeds don't take over.

My grandpa raised cotton in the black lands of north central Texas, and they had to do something called "chopping cotton" to chop all of that Johnson grass out of the root system of the cotton plants.

So, you see, concerning faith, there's a time for breaking up the ground and getting the ground ready. Then there's a time for planting the seed, for maintaining the crop—and then, it's time for harvest! And you have to be able to recognize those times, or you won't reap the harvest.

Similarly, God does not manifest His Presence continually "24–7." Certainly, His Presence is with us continuously. But His Presence isn't in manifestation 24 hours a day, seven days a week, 365 days a year. We have to learn to recognize when the Holy Spirit wants to manifest Himself and then learn to cooperate with Him so He can accomplish what He wants to accomplish in our midst.

I have had people ask me over the years, "What's it like to be the son of Kenneth E. Hagin?"

Many people thought that because Dad ministered under the anointing of the Spirit, he just operated under the anointing all the time.

I would always answer, "Yes, my dad has the power of God with him at all times, but he doesn't operate in that power all the time."

Recognizing the Purpose

The power and Presence of God operates at times and for a purpose. In fact, anytime there is a manifestation of the Presence of God, it's for a purpose!

Let's take the simple gift of prophecy, one of the nine gifts of the Holy Spirit, for example. What is the purpose of that gift? According to the Word of God, it's for edification, exhortation, and comfort (1 Cor. 14:3). That's the purpose or reason why that gift is manifested—for the edification, exhortation, and comfort of the hearers.

Did you know that every meeting and church service also has a purpose? And if it's a healing meeting, then the subject of healing should be preached. My dad always said, "If you want healings, you preach on healing. If you want salvations, you preach on salvation. If you want people to grow up spiritually in the things of God, you preach on those things."

The Bible does say that God confirms His Word with signs following (Mark 16:20). What does God confirm with signs or manifestations of His Presence? *The preaching, teaching, or proclaiming of His Word!*

We have to learn to walk with God in such a way that we can discern His times and purposes. Some have received a little understanding in this area and have run off with it, so to speak, but nothing much came from it, because they didn't have the whole story; they were trying to do things their own way instead of recognizing God's leading and discerning His times and purposes.

If we want to see the greater glory, we are going to have to prayerfully study the subject and learn the operation of the Spirit so that we'll know how to flow with Him in recognizing His times and His purposes. Just as we have to understand how to pray the prayer of faith to receive answered prayer, we must study the operation of the Spirit of God. As we hunger after the things of God and seek to know the ways of His Spirit, I believe we will see greater and greater manifestations of the glory of God in our midst.

Since God created man, He has had people who were willing to carry the torch of His power and demonstrate it to their particular generation. Now, He is looking for people in our generation who are willing to take up the torch and step out of their comfort zone—to step out with nothing under their feet but the Word and the power of God! He has promised to bless them, to anoint them, to send them, and to deliver them. God has promised to give them whatever they need to accomplish His plans in the earth.

Are we willing to take up the torch?

We are not living in these times by chance! God has a plan for the ages and a place for each one of us in His plan. We must begin to stir the embers in our heart as we seek Him diligently. I believe we are the generation that will fan those embers into a bright flame for God!